ORANGE   BLOSSOM
TRAILS

ALSO BY PHILLIP MANNING

*Afoot in the South: Walks in the Natural Areas
of North Carolina*

*Palmetto Journal: Walks in the Natural Areas
of South Carolina*

ORANGE BLOSSOM TRAILS

*Walks in the Natural
Areas of Florida*

PHILLIP   MANNING

Illustrations by
DIANE MANNING

John F. Blair, Publisher
Winston-Salem, North Carolina

DESIGN BY DEBRA LONG HAMPTON AND LIZA LANGRALL
MAPS BY DEBRA LONG HAMPTON
ILLUSTRATIONS BY DIANE MANNING
COVER ILLUSTRATION: DUCK BLIND, CRUICKSHANK TRAIL

*The paper in this book meets the
guidelines for permanence and
durability of the Committee on
Production Guidelines for Book Longevity
of the Council on Library Resources.*

Library of Congress Cataloging-in-Publication Data
Manning, Phillip, 1936–
     Orange blossom trails : walks in the natural areas of Florida /
  Phillip Manning ; illustrations by Diane Manning.
        p.   cm.
     Includes bibliographical references (p.   ) and index.
     ISBN 0-89587-201-3 (alk. paper)
     1. Natural history—Florida—Guidebooks. 2. Natural areas—Florida—
  Guidebooks. 3. Walking—Florida—Guidebooks. 4. Hiking—Florida—
  Guidebooks. 5. Florida—Guidebooks.   I. Title.
  QH105.F6M26   1997
  508.759—dc21   97-25696

Finally, this one's for Diane.

The famous *Orange Grove* commences
about twelve miles south of Gainesville, and extends nearly around
Orange Lake. It is probably the largest
natural orange grove in the world, and
in the spring when the trees are in
blossom, perfumes the whole region.

DANIEL G. BRINTON,
A GUIDE-BOOK OF FLORIDA AND THE SOUTH,
FOR TOURISTS, INVALIDS AND EMIGRANTS, 1869

Panhandle

13

Northeast

Jacksonville

●Pensacola

14 Tallahassee

12

11

16

15

Gainesville

10 9

8

South

1. Victories Big and Small,
   J. N. "Ding" Darling National Wildlife
   Refuge
2. Rock, Water, and Fire,
   Everglades National Park
3. Adventures in Engineering,
   The Middle Keys
4. Birds, Bromeliads, and Field Naturalists,
   Corkscrew Swamp Sanctuary

Central

5. A Varied but Constant Land,
   Myakka River State Park
6. Climbing Elton's Pyramid,
   Lake Kissimmee State Park
7. Life and Death in the Salt Marsh,
   Merritt Island National Wildlife Refuge
8. Big Scrub, Ocala National Forest

Northeast

9. A Walk with Billy, Paynes Prairie State Preserve
10. Old Florida, Manatee Springs State Park
11. Ecology 101, Little Talbot Island State Park
12. Songs of the River, Suwannee River State Park

Panhandle

13. A Forest Redux, Blackwater River State Forest
14. River Bluffs, Ravines, and Disappearing Trees, Torreya State Park
15. Birds, Beasts, and Other Generalists, St. Joseph Peninsula State Park
16. A Resilient Land, St. Marks National Wildlife Refuge

Orlando

7

Central

●Tampa

6

5

South

●Fort Myers

1

4

●Miami

2

3

Contents

Introduction

We left our beat-up rented camper at the campground and strolled into the heart of a cypress swamp on a narrow boardwalk with one worn guardrail. The place was Highlands Hammock State Park; the year was 1966. A campsite cost $2.06 a night, and the campground was nearly empty. Diane and I had our young children, Robin and Michael, with us. We had stopped to watch egrets in the shallows of a dark pond when a big gator surfaced and began to swim steadily toward us. As he closed in, Michael's eyes got big, and he clung tightly to Diane's hand. But Robin backed away from the oncoming gator. Suddenly, there was a splash, and she was gone.

By the time I turned around, all I could see was a small white hand sticking out of the black water. I dropped to the boardwalk and grabbed the hand. When I pulled her to safety, a pen in my shirt pocket fell into the water.

While Diane comforted our wet and frightened daughter, I stuck my arm into the water in a hopeless attempt to reach my brand-new gold ballpoint pen. Gators usually shy away from noisy people, but this one kept coming. When he was a foot or two away, I jerked my arm out of the water and rolled away from the edge of the boardwalk. The gator ignored me and swam on by, but I decided not to jump in after the pen.

Years later, we stopped at the park again. Prices were higher, the campground was full, the boardwalk had two guardrails, and the gator was gone. I peered into the water where I lost the pen, hoping to see a telltale glint, but there was no sign of it.

Florida has boomed since we first visited the state over thirty years ago. The population grew by eight million people between 1960 and 1990, and there are more today. So much has changed in three decades that any recounting of those earlier days smells of nostalgia. But I am not a nostalgic person, and this is not a nostalgic book. It's not about the Florida of the 1960s or even the 1980s. It is about the Florida of today.

One thing that hasn't changed in thirty years is the way I feel about the state. I love it. Or more precisely, I love the natural areas. It's not that I have anything against the rest of the state, but as a naturalist, I am attracted to the wild, so that is where I spend most of my time. And Florida has an abundance of natural areas.

You could count them: one national park, three national forests, ten national wildlife refuges, over one hundred state parks, preserves, and recreation areas. But counting doesn't do them justice. Nor does reciting their names. To appreciate Florida's natural areas, you must visit them.

When you do, it will begin to dawn on you what adding eight million people to the population means. Many campgrounds and picnic areas that were once lightly visited are packed in peak season, and visitor centers at popular parks are mobbed. Amazingly, though, a hiker can still find peace and quiet a hundred yards from most trailheads. On many of the trails in this book, I encountered *no one*. The wonderful loop through the towering slash pines of Long Pine Key in Everglades National Park was completely deserted; Torreya Trail, which takes you into terrain reminiscent of the southern Appalachian Mountains, was empty; not a soul was in sight on the broad white-sand beach at Little Talbot Island; and I saw only red-winged blackbirds and alligators on La Chua Trail at Paynes Prairie.

It's easy to avoid the crowds in Florida's natural areas—all you have to do is walk. You have to stroll the boardwalk among the ancient cypresses at Corkscrew Swamp and wade through wire grass beneath the longleaf pines at Blackwater River. You must poke along and smell the mangrove swamps bordering Wildlife Drive at "Ding" Darling and walk beside the Gulf of Mexico at St. Joseph Peninsula. You have to search for sandhill cranes in the back country at Lake Kissimmee and watch for otters at Myakka River.

I like to walk because I can study and enjoy natural areas without the crowds. But I'm no misanthrope; I wouldn't mind seeing a few more hikers on the trail. We need more people who appreciate wild areas, for these places need our help. Great algae blooms float across Florida Bay, cutting off sunlight and destroying the life beneath them; clear-cutting continues in publicly owned forests, hiding behind the euphemism *regeneration cuts*; and the Keys sag under the weight of unrestrained development.

If more people used natural areas in nonabusive, nonextractive ways—such as hiking, canoeing, and wildlife watching—our remaining wild places would have more supporters. And since we can't go back to the 1960s, that is our best hope for the future: committed people who care about natural areas and are vigilant in defending them.

To galvanize and expand that group of defenders is one reason I wrote this book. But I also wanted to enjoy myself and to suggest places where others could enjoy themselves. Consequently, I hope to see some newcomers the next time I walk one of these trails. And if any of you should run across a badly tarnished gold pen at Highlands Hammock, let me know. Perhaps I *am* a little nostalgic, because I'd still like to get it back.

Peninsular Florida is a flat bed of limestone covered with a sheet of sand. The Panhandle has some relief, but the highest point in the state is only 345 feet above sea level. Compared to other Southern states, Florida is a distressingly uniform place with poor soil. The result should be a few ecosystems with a small number of plant and animal species.

That, however, is not the case. Florida has at least a dozen major ecosystems, from temperate hardwood forests to salt marshes, from scrub to swamps. (For more detail, see *Ecosystems of Florida*, edited by Ronald L. Myers and John J. Jewel.) It also has a greater variety of wildlife and plants than any other Southern state.

One reason for this variety is climate. The state's high rainfall and humidity produce a profusion of plant life, and its temperature gradient—from temperate in the north to tropical in the south—encourages diversity. Another reason is the state's limestone bed. Although it appears to be solid, the rock substrate actually resembles a prairie-dog town, riddled with tunnels and pockets. The high water table turns these cavities into water-filled caverns and underground streams. The subterranean water often reaches the surface as artesian springs. These nooks and crannies and springs have their own biota, as do the dunes, beaches, and saltwater marshes along the coast. Together, they yield a farrago of rich natural areas that makes Florida a naturalist's dream.

As diverse as the state is, though, it falls within only one physiographic region: the coastal plain. Thus, there is no straightforward way to group its ecosystems. For the purposes of this book, I have divided the state into regions based on location: south, central, northeast, and Panhandle.

The southern region is that part of the state south of the northern shore of Lake Okeechobee; the central region lies between Ocala and Okeechobee; the Panhandle and the northeastern region are north of Ocala and separated by a north-south line that passes through Madison and meets the Gulf of Mexico near Steinhatchee. These regions are arbitrary, but they should help you select your walks.

As in the previous two books in this series, each chapter is composed of three parts and concerns itself with one walk. The first part consists of a map, directions to the trailhead, a brief description of the route, the length of the walk, and its degree of difficulty (from "easy" to "moderate" to "strenuous"). The second part describes the walk and the terrain through which it passes. It also tells of historical events that shaped the land and made it what it is today. The third section gives the information you will need to take the walks yourself—whom to write or call, where to stay—and a bibliography.

Most of these walks are on trails that are safer than the sidewalks of most cities. But you can still get lost or develop a blister or fall off a boardwalk. At one time or another, you will almost certainly be bitten by mosquitoes or ticks or no-see-ums. So even though natural areas are not unusually dangerous places, it does make sense to take a few precautions.

If I walk alone, I always let someone know where I am going and when I expect to be back. I also take a few safety-related items in my pack:

* Map
* Compass
* Band-Aids
* Pocketknife
* Insect repellent
* Skin-So-Soft (for no-see-ums)
* Two full water bottles
* Waterproof matches
* Waterproof windbreaker
* Bandanna or handkerchief
* Aspirin or ibuprofen

This list is almost identical to those in the earlier books of this series, and aside from the water, all the items on it weigh only a pound or two. Together, they cost less than a hundred dollars.

SOUTH

Here is in this river and in the waters all over Florida, a very curious and handsome bird, the people call them Snake Birds.

WILLIAM BARTRAM, 1791

Victories Big and Small

Indigo Trail
J. N. "Ding" Darling National Wildlife Refuge

The main tract of the 6,000-acre J. N. "Ding" Darling National Wildlife Refuge is on Sanibel Island, about 15 miles southwest of Fort Myers. From Fort Myers, take S.R. 867 across the San Carlos Bay Causeway to Periwinkle Way on Sanibel. Proceed west on Periwinkle Way to Palm Ridge Road, which takes you to Sanibel-Captiva Road. The refuge's visitor center and parking lot are on the right just off Sanibel-Captiva Road.

The first leg of the walk is on Wildlife Drive, a 5-mile one-way shell road that runs through the refuge. After 2 miles, and about 100 yards before the road reaches a wildlife observation tower, Cross Dike Trail leads west to Indigo Trail, which curls southeast back to the trailhead.

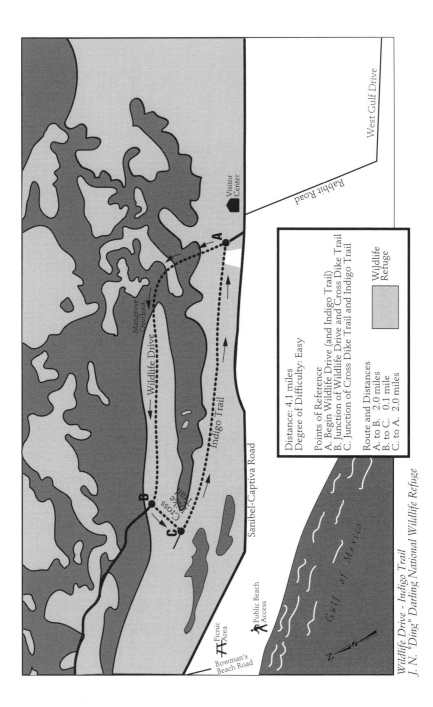

Wildlife Drive - Indigo Trail
J. N. "Ding" Darling National Wildlife Refuge

Distance: 4.1 miles
Degree of Difficulty: Easy

Points of Reference
A. Begin Wildlife Drive (and Indigo Trail)
B. Junction of Wildlife Drive and Cross Dike Trail
C. Junction of Cross Dike Trail and Indigo Trail

Route and Distances
A. to B.   2.0 miles
B. to C.   0.1 mile
C. to A.   2.0 miles

Wildlife Refuge

We first visited Sanibel Island over twenty-five years ago, but I remember those lazy days clearly. Every afternoon about an hour before sunset, the eight-foot-long bull alligator in the pond behind the trim white cottage my family and I were renting would slide up on the grassy bank to soak up a few rays before nightfall. Traffic on the sandy road beside the pond was light and alligators were common, so no one but me paid much attention. I liked to stroll down to the pond and sit in a rickety plastic lawn chair and watch him as the light faded and the air cooled.

Since those days, Sanibel has changed predictably: the cottage is gone, replaced by ritzy condominiums, and so is the pond. In its place is a man-made "natural area" that includes a tiny lily-pad-covered pool that no self-respecting gator would be caught dead in. But despite the tidal wave of development that swamped the island (and continues to this day), Sanibel's one great natural area has remained pretty much unchanged in the last twenty-five years; in fact, if anything, J. N. "Ding" Darling National Wildlife Refuge appears to be attracting more wildlife than ever.

Sanibel Island is shaped like a shallow **U** or a parenthesis lying on its back. To the north are San Carlos Bay and the mouth of the Caloosahatchee River; to the south are the turquoise waters of the Gulf of Mexico. The wildlife refuge covers much of the northern side of the **U**, and it offers the best birding I have ever encountered. Over two hundred species have been spotted here, many of which are uncommon elsewhere: roseate spoonbills and mottled ducks, ground doves and anis, wood storks and swallow-tailed kites.

Variety is not the only thing that makes "Ding" Darling such a great spot for birders, though; the birds here seem more *accessible* than those at other wildlife refuges. So easy are they to approach that they appear to be posing for the tourists that cruise Wildlife Drive, the main road through the refuge.

I start walking down Wildlife Drive on a warm, cloudless April morning. The road is broad and sandy and thankfully devoid of cars this early in the day. The canal is a "borrow ditch," a ditch dug to provide soil for other purposes, in this case the dike on which the roadway was built in 1962.

The road passes to the right of a large impoundment that formed when the dike was built. This impoundment is the only place I have ever observed the underwater fishing technique of a cormorant.

As I stood on the bank a few years back, a double-crested cormorant paddled by about fifty feet from shore, then dove beneath the surface of the clear water. Like a torpedo, it barreled straight toward me, then darted among the mangrove roots, swerving first this way and then that, propelling itself with oversized webbed feet, chasing and finally catching a small fish not five feet from me.

Though the cormorant drew my eye, the roots among which it pursued its prey are far more important to Sanibel. In this eco-system, the heavy lifting is done by mangroves.

Sanibel is a young island. It started five thousand years ago as a sand bar, an accretive afterthought attached to Captiva Island, its northern neighbor. (Sanibel and Captiva, now joined by a bridge, became two islands about a thousand years ago.) It is likely that the first plant to establish itself on the drying sand was a mangrove.

Mangroves are a group of salt-tolerant plants and trees found in the tropics and subtropics. Though they can grow in fresh water, they are unable to compete with freshwater plants and trees, so they are almost invariably found near salt or brackish water. Three species flourish in the sandy, salty soil of Sanibel: the colorfully named red, black, and white mangroves. The buttonwood, often found in close association with mangroves, is also abundant here.

The first mangrove on the sand spit that became Sanibel was probably a red mangrove (*Rhizophora mangle*), the most adventuresome of the bunch. Even today, lonesome red mangroves can be seen growing on sand bars far from the nearest land. The red mangrove is easily recognized by the tangled system of prop roots that supports it. It is an evergreen shrub or small tree, but aside from its roots, its most distinctive part is its fruit.

It begins as an undistinguished brown, egg-shaped berry an inch or two long. But the berries germinate while still attached to the tree. The result is a ten-inch-long, cigar-shaped seedling called a propagule, which drops from the tree and floats vertically in the water. When the propagule encounters something solid, it puts down roots, attaches itself to the bottom, and—*voilà!*—a tiny red mangrove appears in the water. The mangrove's prop roots trap mud and silt, and invertebrates cling to the roots.

The accumulation stabilizes the bottom, and an ecosystem begins to form. If the pioneer is not washed away by turbulent seas or the wake of a powerboat, a mangrove colony develops and—if accompanied by sedimentation or a change in sea level—an island emerges from the sea.

Similar processes must have raised Sanibel from the waters of San Carlos Bay. And though the island has matured and other plants and trees have invaded it (or have been imported by humans), Sanibel is still basically a mangrove swamp.

Farther on, I spot the first black mangroves (*Avicennia germinans*) in the shallow waters of an impoundment. The species is similar to the red variety, but it lacks prop roots. Even without prop roots, though, black mangroves are easy to identify: they send up short breathing roots, or pneumatophores, which look like colonies of oversized black pencils stuck in the mud beneath the trees.

I've never seen this impoundment when it wasn't packed with birds, especially at low tide, and today is no exception. Several white ibises and a little blue heron are feeding near its center, and an anhinga dries its wings in the mangroves bordering the dike. A great egret stands white and still near the canal, and a reddish egret dances in the shallow water, scaring up its next meal. A great blue heron flies overhead and lights on the shore.

The first car of the day cruises by, its tires raising a cloud of dust. Its windows are up and the air conditioning is apparently on, even though the weather is perfect, the temperature in the low seventies. The car slows as it passes the impoundment but does not stop. This is not uncommon; of the 750,000 people who visit the refuge each year, most confine their activities to a drive down this five-mile one-way road, and many *never* stop.

At "Ding" Darling, wildlife is everywhere, and I used to wonder what these sightseers were looking for. After many trips through the refuge, I learned the answer: alligators. Though the day of the backyard gator is mostly gone from Sanibel, the species has rebounded from overhunting, so gators are plentiful at "Ding" Darling. Even the most jaded tourist will stop to gawk at them, often backing up traffic on Wildlife Drive. But as interesting as the gators are, it's sad to see so many people drive past the rest of the refuge's astonishing array of wildlife.

I continue north on Wildlife Drive. Sunlight glints on water on both sides of the road, shimmering surfaces peppered with islands where tall palmettos grow among low mangroves. The air has a tangy, sour smell, one of salt water and swamp. A mullet jumps in the bay to my right, and a woodpecker hammers away in the distance. A ray swims lazily in the clear, brackish water of the impoundment, and an osprey circles overhead.

The osprey (*Pandion haliaetus*) is one of the environmental movement's biggest victories, and its presence is a tribute to Rachel Carson, one of our country's great environmentalists. When I first visited "Ding" Darling in 1969, I didn't see a single osprey. Not only were they rare here, they were rare everywhere else in the United States, too. The culprit was DDT, a pesticide that thinned ospreys' (and other birds') eggshells, making them easy to break. The decrease in chicks caused osprey populations to plummet. After the publication of *Silent Spring*, Carson's 1962 indictment of pesticides in general and DDT in particular, DDT use was banned in the United States, halting the osprey's plunge toward extirpation.

Two years after that first visit, I saw an osprey at the refuge, and

by the late 1970s, almost forty pairs were nesting on Sanibel. Since then, the Fish and Wildlife Service has erected nesting platforms in the refuge, and ospreys are now as common as blue jays.

The air grows warmer, and there is no breeze. More cars pass, and a film of white dust coats the leaves of the mangroves and sea grapes that grow beside the road. A sharp *keeyer, keeyer* comes from one of the roadside trees. I'm no expert on bird calls, but I know this one. I also know where to find the bird; I saw a red-shouldered hawk at this same spot last year. Sure enough, just a few yards ahead, a hawk is perched in the low branches of a buttonwood tree. I don't know if it's the same bird I saw before, but it's certainly the same species, and it's in the same place.

Buteo lineatus is another species that is recovering from pesticide-related population decline. It is a large hawk with a pale red chest barred with white. Its tail is marked with alternating bands of white and black. The red-shouldered hawk gets its common name from the rufous patches on its shoulders, which are almost impossible to see when the bird is above you, as it almost always is. Red-shouldered hawks seem to tolerate people better than most hawks, and this particular bird tolerates me better than most red-shouldered hawks. Last year, I got quite close to where he or she was perching. (Except for a slight difference in size, male and female red-shouldered hawks are almost identical in appearance, at least to humans.)

I move forward slowly. Its perch is only twenty feet above the ground, and I am only a few feet from the perch. It is a beautiful bird, with a red breast and fierce, uncompromising eyes. It ignores me as I ease my tape recorder out of my pocket.

Every now and then, as I walk through the natural areas I write about, it occurs to me that I ought to do something more *useful.* Not just take in the sights and record what I see, not just dig into the history of the land and write about it, but do something *really* useful, like add pertinent observations to the scientific literature. As I watch the hawk, it dawns on me that this may be my chance. What ornithologist wouldn't like to study a red-shouldered hawk up close in the wild?

I stand poised, ready to record what happens. Minutes pass and *nothing happens.* Birds call in the distance, pelicans sail overhead, and cars speed by. A silvery layer of dust begins to form on my skin. And still the hawk stares straight ahead and does absolutely *nothing*! After ten minutes or so, a young woman stops her car and comes over to see what I'm looking at. The bird shakes its head slightly, as if annoyed, then flies off across the impoundment. I look at my tape recorder, into which I have uttered not a word since I spotted the hawk. "Red-shouldered hawk," I say into it. "No pertinent observations. Forget career in ornithology."

Wildlife Drive continues northwest, flat and hot. A boardwalk leads to the right. The weathered boards end at a low platform overlooking a broad arm of San Carlos Bay. Tree crabs swarm through the mangroves beside the boardwalk, and snowy egrets prance in the shallows. It was here that I saw my first "Ding" Darling osprey. The year was 1971, and the species was just beginning to recover from the reckless spraying of pesticides, but I was about to find out that DDT was not the only man-made threat to ospreys.

At first, I wasn't sure what I was seeing. Finally, I made it out: a single huge wing flapping in the water, a wing seemingly without a body. It soon became apparent what had happened: an osprey had stooped on a fish and entangled itself in a fishing net. Its one loose wing was beating the water as the bird tried to free itself.

I was absolutely helpless. The bird was at least a quarter of a mile from me. Without a boat, there was no way I could get to it. And because I was on foot, I couldn't contact refuge officials in time for them to help. All I could do was watch as the wing beat slowed and finally stopped. As I was leaving, the wing rose slowly out of the water and flapped a few more times. That osprey is the only bird I have ever dreamed about, and what I see in my dream is one powerful, disembodied wing splashing forever in gray-green water.

Not far beyond the boardwalk, the road intersects Cross Dike Trail, a short path that leads to Indigo Trail, which I plan to follow back to the visitor center. Before taking it, though, I walk a few hundred yards farther down Wildlife Drive to an observation tower. I don't climb the tower but veer to the right side of the road to scan a mangrove-rimmed pond. Sure enough, a flock of roseate spoonbills is feeding near the mangroves. I count twenty-seven, an unusually high number.

Roseate spoonbills (*Ajaia ajaja*) are common at "Ding" Darling in the spring. Though they can be found anywhere on the refuge, I've rarely missed seeing them at this particular pond, probably because they roost at night in the mangroves bordering it.

Spoonbills are large, awkward-looking birds with stiltlike legs, spoonlike bills, featherless heads, and shocking pink wings. Unlike herons and egrets, they do not find their prey by sight. Instead, they feed by touch, sweeping their long, flat bills through the water and clamping down on any small fish or crustaceans they encounter. A flock of feeding spoonbills is truly an odd sight, a gaggle of pink bodies wading in shallow water on improbably skinny legs, heads down, sweeping left and right, left and right.

Around the beginning of this century, plume hunters nearly wiped out the roseate spoonbill in this country. The huge colonies that once nested along the Gulf coast from Florida to Texas dropped to twenty-five or so pairs that held out in the remote swamps at the southernmost tip of Florida. Just as the ospreys and hawks needed Rachel Carson, the spoonbills needed a champion. One showed up in 1902 in the form of the newly created Audubon Society. The society posted wardens in Texas and southern Florida to protect spoonbills and other wading birds. Roseate spoonbills from Mexico began to recolonize Texas, and the number of birds along the edge of Florida Bay started to grow. By 1992, over six thousand roseate spoonbills nested in the United States.

I backtrack to Cross Dike Trail, which leads away from the traffic on Wildlife Drive to Indigo Trail. It is quiet here, the trail deserted. Two ground doves, lovely sparrow-sized birds with rufous-tipped wings, peck in the dust of the path. Three mottled ducks fly from the marshes on the southern side of the trail toward the impoundments.

The empty trail stretches in front of me. It passes mangroves, palmettos, gumbo limbos, and occasional expanses of water. An osprey platform stands beside the trail. A single osprey perches on it, clutching a fish in its talons. I lengthen my stride and enjoy the simple rhythm of walking.

About halfway back, the trees disappear and the country opens up. Tiny white wildflowers carpet the ground. It's a wild and lovely landscape, and it reminds me of the debt we owe another environmentalist (or conservationist, as they were called in the days before Rachel Carson), the person who more than any other was responsible for saving this land from developers, and for whom the refuge is named.

Jay Norwood Darling spent much of life as a political cartoonist for the *Des Moines Register and Leader*, winning two Pulitzer Prizes for his work. He acquired the nickname "Ding" while he was in college and never lost it. He was a man of contrasts: an ardent conservationist and a conservative Republican; an excellent artist and an able administrator who ran the United States Biological Survey (the predecessor of the Fish and Wildlife Service) for almost two years under President Franklin Roosevelt. While he was with the Biological Survey, Darling added four million acres to the national wildlife refuge system; he also started the duck-stamp program and designed the first one.

In 1936, Darling visited Captiva Island, which had a permanent population of forty-five at the time, and fell in love with the place. It was the best thing that could have happened to Sanibel and Captiva. In 1939, Darling was instrumental in getting the state of Florida to designate the islands as refuges for wildlife. Then, in 1945, the federal government established Sanibel National Wildlife Refuge, which was later enlarged thanks to the efforts of the Sanibel-Captiva Audubon Society. Five years after his death in 1962, the refuge was renamed the J. N. "Ding" Darling National Wildlife Refuge.

In his later years, Ding became discouraged with Florida politics and sold his home on Captiva. Biographer David L. Lendt quotes him as saying that Florida "comes nearer being blind in both eyes to its wildlife and fish endowment than any state in the union." It was the sentiment of one who had fought the good fight and believed he had lost.

But Ding hadn't lost. Though condos are still going up on Sanibel and Captiva, alligators, ospreys, red-shouldered hawks, and roseate spoonbills are back at the refuge in good numbers. Furthermore, the citizens of Florida, after years of legislative foot-dragging, voted overwhelmingly in 1994 to amend their constitution to ban the use of entanglement nets in salt or brackish water anywhere in the state. It was a victory for the state's environmentalists, perhaps not as big as banning DDT or establishing this refuge or protecting alligators and roseate spoonbills from hunters, but important nonetheless.

It was important to me, too. With luck, I'll never dream again of standing helplessly on a platform while one huge wing futilely beats the waters of San Carlos Bay.

BEFORE YOU GO

For More Information
J. N. "Ding" Darling National Wildlife Refuge
1 Wildlife Drive
Sanibel, FL 33957
(813) 472-1100

Accommodations
An astounding array of hotels, motels, and condominiums is available on Sanibel and Captiva. Contact

Sanibel and Captiva Islands Chamber of Commerce
P.O. Box 166

Sanibel, FL 33957
(813) 472-1080

Campgrounds

Camping is not permitted at the refuge. Sanibel and Captiva have no public and only one privately owned campground. The nearest public campground is Koreshan State Historic Site, near Estero. For information, contact

Koreshan State Historic Site
P.O. Box 7
Estero, FL 33928
(813) 992-0311

Maps

Wildlife Drive, Cross Dike Trail, and Indigo Trail are well marked and easy to follow. The map in the refuge's free brochure is all that's needed for this walk.

Fees

The refuge charges a fee at the entrance to Wildlife Drive—$4 for a car and $1 per person for walkers and bicyclists.

Special Precautions

The refuge is open from sunrise to sunset every day except Friday, when Wildlife Drive is closed. Even on Friday, however, Indigo Trail is open to hikers.

J. N. "Ding" Darling National Wildlife Refuge is one of the buggiest spots in Florida, and therefore in the world. In fact, the original purpose of the dike on which Wildlife Drive was built was not to accommodate hordes of tourists but to control hordes of mosquitoes. Before the mosquito-control program, a single light trap on Sanibel caught nearly 400,000 mosquitoes in one night. There are fewer mosquitoes these days, but only those people with a death wish should walk in the refuge without taking mosquito repellent with them. No-see-ums also love "Ding" Darling. The only repellent that has worked for me is Avon's Skin-So-Soft.

Points of Interest

To get into the heart of a mangrove swamp, the refuge offers two canoe trails: the 2-mile Commodore Creek Canoe Trail and the 4-mile Buck Creek Canoe Trail. Rental canoes are available for both trails.

Additional Reading

Ding: The Life of Jay Norwood Darling by David L. Lendt, Iowa State University Press, Ames, Iowa, 1979.

Florida: A Guide to the Southernmost State, compiled and written by the Federal Writers' Project of the Work Projects Administration, Oxford University Press, New York, 1939.

The Nature of Things on Sanibel, revised edition, by George R. Campbell, Pineapple Press, Sarasota, 1988.

"Roseate Redux" by David E. Manry, *Birder's World* 9, February 1995, 22–27.

The Seashell Islands: A History of Sanibel and Captiva by Elinore Mayer Dormer, Vantage Press, New York, 1975.

Silent Spring by Rachel Carson, Houghton Mifflin Company, New York, 1962. A true classic.

Rock, Water, and Fire

Gumbo Limbo and Long Pine Key Trails
Everglades National Park

The main entrance to the 1.5-million-acre Everglades National Park is a few miles west of Florida City (just south of Homestead) on S.R. 9336.

This walk starts at the Royal Palm Visitor Center, 4 miles from the park entrance. Proceed clockwise on the paved, easy-to-follow Gumbo Limbo Trail. Near the end of the trail, a grassy road lined with royal palms leads west to Hidden Lake. Just beyond the lake, the path intersects Old Ingraham Highway, which is closed to cars. Walk north on the old highway to Research Road, then west to Gate 2. The 2.5-mile Long Pine Key loop begins there and ends back on Research Road at Gate 2A. From there, retrace your footsteps to the Royal Palm Visitor Center.

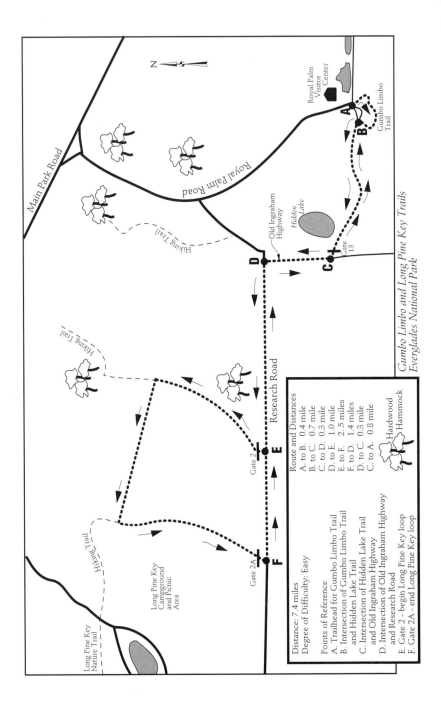

Gumbo Limbo and Long Pine Key Trails
Everglades National Park

Route and Distances	
A. to B.	0.4 mile
B. to C.	0.7 mile
C. to D.	0.3 mile
D. to E.	1.0 mile
E. to F.	2.5 miles
F. to D.	1.4 miles
D. to C.	0.3 mile
C. to A.	0.8 mile

Distance: 7.4 miles
Degree of Difficulty: Easy

Points of Reference
A. Trailhead for Gumbo Limbo Trail
B. Intersection of Gumbo Limbo Trail
   and Hidden Lake Trail
C. Intersection of Hidden Lake Trail
   and Old Ingraham Highway
D. Intersection of Old Ingraham Highway
   and Research Road
E. Gate 2 - begin Long Pine Key loop
F. Gate 2A - end Long Pine Key loop

ROCK, WATER, AND FIRE

Real nature resembles the nature programs on television the way a real courtroom trial resembles a *Perry Mason* episode. Real nature, like a real trial, is subtle and reserved, even slow. As author Bill McKibben points out in *The Age of Missing Information*, real nature moves at the pace of life, not at the frantic speed of entertainment. In real nature, you can walk all day before you glimpse a hawk; you can spend days in the woods before you get close to one and weeks before you see one stoop. On television, you can push a button on your remote and find a hawk perched in a tree seemingly a few feet away from your armchair, then watch as it stoops and nails its prey—all in thirty seconds.

Occasionally, though, nature surprises you with a burst of television-like action. It happened to me one day on the Old Ingraham Highway near Hidden Lake in Everglades National Park. I had been prowling the area for hours and had seen lots of butterflies—viceroys and sulfurs and long wings—but nothing prepared me for the moment when I stepped off the road into some low brush. Two dozen or more long wings—zebras and oranges—suddenly swirled up from the ground and enveloped me in a shimmering cloak of black and white and bright copper. If a television cameraman had been along, I would have had my fifteen minutes—or at least fifteen seconds—of fame.

It was a rare experience, one I'll remember long after the last nature program on television has slipped from my mind. But if the experience was rare, those brightly hued butterflies weren't. This is an exotic land filled with exotic life.

On a winter morning a few days later, Diane and I leave the bright sunlight of the Royal Palm Visitor Center for Gumbo Limbo Trail. Immediately, we are enclosed in a cloistered, green forest, shady and choked with vegetation. It's the kind of jungly place W. H. Hudson must have had in mind when he named his romantic novel of South America *Green Mansions*.

Some of the vegetation here is tropical, but some of it can be found in temperate climates. The grapevines, Virginia creepers, and morning glories beside the path occur all over the South, as do the poison-ivy vines climbing the trunks of hardwood trees. The coral beans along the trail are found throughout Florida, as are the live oaks and the resurrection ferns that cling to their massive limbs.

Slowly, though, one begins to notice the unusual. Air plants grow exuberantly on almost every tree. Massive strangler figs wrap themselves around their hosts. Soon, the path passes a gumbo limbo, the tree for which the trail was named. And one glance at *it* is enough to convince tourists from colder climates that they aren't in Kansas anymore.

The gumbo limbo, *Bursera simaruba*, is a large, red hulk of a tree

found throughout the West Indies and the Caribbean. The common name, of Bantu origin, means "birdlime," a reference to the glue that African slaves made from its sap to coat tree branches to capture birds. In the United States, the gumbo limbo occurs as far north as Tampa, but it can withstand only occasional light frosts, so it is more plentiful in southern Florida and the Keys. Because of its red, peeling bark, the gumbo limbo is sometimes called the "sunburn tree" or the "tourist tree."

Unlike many tropical trees, the gumbo limbo is deciduous. It loses its leaves in early spring, but new growth follows so quickly that it appears evergreen. This capacity for rapid regeneration makes the gumbo limbo an easy tree to propagate: plant a limb and roots will form, producing a new tree. On some Caribbean islands, thick gumbo limbo branches are used as fence posts, which eventually results in rows of shiny, red trees with wire strung between them.

Midway through Gumbo Limbo Trail, the path enters a forest of sprawling live oaks. Orchids, resurrection ferns, and other epiphytes cling to every branch. Colorful zebra long wings and viceroys flutter through the understory. Among the oaks stand papayas and royal palms, and woodpeckers call in the distance. The entire trail is paved, but the ground beside it is harder than the asphalt in places. Only a thin layer of soil supports this great forest, and gray bedrock shows through in places where the organic skin has worn away.

"To understand the Everglades," wrote Marjory Stoneman Douglas in her 1947 classic, *The Everglades: River of Grass*, "one must first understand the rock." To understand the rock, one must realize that southern Florida has been underwater for most of its geologic life. The early seas laid down thick layers of limestone. About twenty-five million years ago, Florida began to emerge from the water, but it continued to undergo periodic immersions when sea levels rose. South of Lake Okeechobee, this limestone table (known as the Floridan Plateau) is so flat that the only way to tell downhill is by watching which way the water flows. Thus, when Lake Okeechobee overflowed during the rainy seasons of spring and summer, a shallow sheet of fresh water fifty or more miles wide flowed sluggishly southward from the lake toward Florida Bay. The saw-grass marsh that developed on this periodically flooded limestone table was the Everglades, Douglas's "River of Grass."

Throughout the Everglades, patches of limestone bedrock are visible where the soil has been washed or blown away. In places, steep-sided rock pits known as "solution holes" pock the bedrock. The holes form when water—made acidic by organic matter— seeps through fissures in the bedrock and dissolves the underlying limestone. Eventually, the surface rock collapses into the cavity, leaving a solution hole.

Near the end of Gumbo Limbo Trail, we follow a grassy road that leads out of the thick, green tangle of Royal Palm Hammock into a flat prairie, bright in the morning sun. Wild tamarinds and century plants line the road. An iridescent blue dragonfly hunts insects in the underbrush, and an anhinga sails overhead, its improbably long neck fully extended. To the north is blank, gray flatness, relieved by only an occasional royal palm. This is the saw-grass prairie, the terrain for which Everglades National Park was named.

Just beyond Hidden Lake, the road intersects the Old Ingraham Highway, and we walk north on it toward Research Road. Orange and zebra long wings float by on narrow, delicate wings. Viceroys and Gulf fritillaries sip nectar from small flowers beside the road. I step into the brush, hoping for a rerun of my earlier experience, but all I scare up today is one small sulfur.

The Old Ingraham Highway was built in 1922. It was the first land link to Flamingo, the southernmost town in peninsular Florida and, in my opinion, the buggiest. In the old days, residents of the town dressed in heavy clothes and wore netted hats. Every house had a smudge pot, and the rooms were blackened by soot from their constant use. Even livestock had to be kept in screened pens. One journalist reported in 1893 that he saw an oil lamp extinguished by a swarm of mosquitoes. I've never seen the mosquitoes *that* thick in Flamingo, but when the wind lays at sunset, I have watched black clouds of them envelop men and women, causing them to shriek and run for shelter.

The idea behind the Old Ingraham Highway was to provide easier access to Flamingo to help the town develop. In fact, the population dwindled, as residents used the new road to leave. Today, Flamingo is part of the national park, and time has erased most signs of the old fishing village. The flamingos for which the town was named are rarely seen these days, but the mosquitoes are still around to remind us of the past.

The Old Ingraham Highway ends at Research Road. We turn

west, walking on the road's wide shoulder to Gate 2. Beyond the gate is Long Pine Key. The scattered tall pines and low underbrush are similar to the longleaf-pine savannas of northern Florida, but ecologists call this area a "southern Florida rockland." It contains one of the most interesting, least-advertised ecosystems in the Everglades. To understand why this ecosystem developed here, one must, as before, first understand the rock.

Though the ground here appears absolutely flat, it isn't. Both Long Pine Key and Royal Palm Hammock sit on a ridge of limestone known as the Miami rock ridge. The ridge began to form over one hundred thousand years ago, when pellets of limestone started precipitating out of the shallow, mineral-rich seas covering southern Florida. The deposits are called oolitic limestone, or oolite, because the pellets resemble tiny fish eggs. The deposits grew over the millennia and formed a wide ridge that starts in Miami and runs south to Homestead, then west into the Everglades. (Another ridge of Miami oolite starts at Big Pine Key and runs to Key West.) When the ocean receded, exposure to air hardened the surface of the oolite, which, when eroded by water, forms the karstic landscape visible along the trail.

As ridges go, the Miami rock ridge isn't much; it rises only a few feet above the saw-grass marsh. But in the Everglades, even an inch or two in elevation makes a difference. The reason is that great, wide, shallow sheet of water that used to slop over the southern lip of Lake Okeechobee.

Under natural conditions, the roots of the saw grass in the Everglades are wet for about ten months a year. The depth of the water, though, rarely exceeds one foot. The pines (and the other vegetation on Long Pine Key) prosper only on dry ground and in places where flooding is infrequent and shallow, conditions found in Everglades National Park only on the Miami rock ridge.

Leathery bracken and coontie line the rocky path that takes us into the pinelands. Above them is an understory of saw palmettos, wild tamarinds, and tetrazygia. Widely dispersed slash pines with imposing orange-flecked trunks tower over the brush. Some of the pines, snapped off twenty or thirty feet above the ground, serve as reminders that Hurricane Andrew blew through here a few years ago.

The ground is hard, solid rock in places, and the walking is easy. We soon reach a cutoff trail that leads west, and we follow it toward Long Pine Key Campground. Butterflies and dragonflies zip through the underbrush. A two-inch-long dragonfly lights on a bush near the trail and stays there long enough for me to get a look at it. It has orange-and-black wings and a head that is all eyes. It is a Halloween pennant, *Celithemis eponina*, and like the rest of the dragonflies, it is my kind of bug.

Dragonflies have bulging compound eyes that let them see in almost every direction, including behind them. This allows them to easily spot small flying insects, their preferred prey. In the Everglades, many of the small flying insects they spot are mosquitoes, and anything that eats mosquitoes is my friend. I toy briefly with the idea of importing dragonflies to Flamingo but dismiss the notion. Flamingo mosquitoes are so numerous and so big that they would probably eat the dragonflies.

Before we reach the campground, the trail turns south, back toward Research Road. Huge thistles and varnish bushes and wild lantanas grow beside the path. Deer tracks dimple a rare patch of sand. These pinelands were once home to the Florida panther, but only a few—if any—still survive here, and your chance of seeing one is about as good as winning the lottery. But what you will see, what dominates this landscape, are the tall, long-needled slash pines.

These are not ordinary slash pines, *Pinus elliottii*. These are a subspecies, *P. elliottii* var. *densa*, also known as Dade County pine. Because of its unusually high resin content, Dade County pine is hard, dense, and termite-resistant. Since these are exactly the properties one would like in a building material, Dade County pine was the wood preferred by early homebuilders in southern Florida. Consequently, much of the pinelands of southern Florida are gone, and it's reassuring to have this remnant protected by the national park. Without that protection, Dade County pines would likely be as rare as panthers.

At Research Road, we retrace our footsteps toward Royal Palm Hammock, which looms in the distance. The densely wooded hammock also sits on the Miami rock ridge. Why a hammock there and pinelands here? The answer is fire. Without fire, Long Pine Key would become a hardwood hammock in two or three decades. Fires kill the hardwoods that would eventually take over the pinelands, but they spare most of the fire-resistant pines.

When these ecosystems formed, lightning took care of the periodic burning. Where fires were common, pinelands developed. Where they were uncommon—downwind of a marsh, for example—hardwood hammocks developed. Today, the National Park Service provides the sparks that keep these pinelands pinelands.

Maintaining the pinewoods is, unfortunately, only a minor victory for the park service. Much of Everglades National Park is
saw-grass marsh. And the marsh is drying up. The pinelands of
Long Pine Key are entirely inside the park and are managed by
the park service, but the water the Everglades so desperately needs
comes from outside the park, from the aforementioned Lake
Okeechobee, the largest natural lake in the southern United States.

Marjory Stoneman Douglas says that men first began to mon-
key around with the Everglades' plumbing in 1882, when a canal
was dug to connect the westward-flowing Caloosahatchie River
to Lake Okeechobee. The canal created an unrestricted outlet from
the lake to the Gulf of Mexico. Later, other canals were dug in
the Everglades, diverting water to the Atlantic coast and creating
huge tracts of dry land for growing sugarcane and other crops.
Finally, a levee was built around the southern end of Lake
Okeechobee to stop the flooding that provided the Everglades
with water. Today, the only outlets from the lake are canals, whose
gates are raised and lowered more to suit the demands of agriculture than the needs of the saw-grass marsh and its inhabitants.

It's true that we have made a mess of this once-great ecosystem. Hundreds of newspaper and magazine articles have been
written about the deteriorating state of the Everglades—for a particularly pessimistic assessment, read Joy Williams's "The Imaginary Everglades" in the January 1994 issue of *Outside*—and numerous organizations have been founded to try to protect what's
left, including Douglas's own Friends of the Everglades.

Most of the articles are on the money. Breeding water-bird
counts have plummeted since the 1930s, and the fishing isn't what
it used to be. Introduced plants such as melaleuca and Brazilian
pepper have spread across the land like wildfire in the pinelands,
choking out native vegetation. Algal blooms float across Florida

Bay because of the reduced flow of fresh water from the Everglades. (For more about this, see the next chapter, "Adventures in Engineering.") There is no doubt: the Everglades aren't what they used to be, and they are continuing to decline.

But they do still exist, and the packed parking lots at visitor centers attest to the park's popularity. Surprisingly, except for the very short, very popular Anhinga Trail (see the "Before You Go" section of this chapter), the footpaths of Everglades National Park are deserted. On our walk through Long Pine Key, we saw not one soul. So don't let pessimistic articles or the park's popularity stop you from visiting and hiking here. It is an endlessly fascinating destination with oddball trees, colorful insects, and rare mammals.

But every visitor should also remember the rest of the story: this is an ecosystem headed in the wrong direction. So in addition to enjoying what is here, you might consider trying to help correct the problems besieging the park. One way to do this is to get involved with Douglas's Friends of the Everglades or one of the other groups that aim to restore the water flow the park so desperately needs. After all, if you don't participate in saving the Everglades, the only Everglades left will be on nature television. And as much fun as that is, it doesn't compare to the real thing.

BEFORE YOU GO

■

For More Information
Everglades National Park
40001 State Road 9336
Homestead, FL 33034
(305) 242-7700

Accommodations
Four entrances lead into the park. The Florida City entrance, just south of Homestead, is only 4 miles from the Royal Palm Visitor Center, where this walk starts. Motels are available in Florida City and Homestead. Contact

Homestead–Florida City Chamber of Commerce
43 North Krone Avenue
Homestead, FL 33030
(305) 247-2332

An alternative is to stay in Flamingo. The Flamingo Lodge offers back-country boat tours, a marina, two restaurants, and a variety of rooms and cottages. I like the place because of the way some folks dress for dinner: long-sleeved shirts and camouflage pants topped with floppy hats and mosquito netting. Somehow, I feel right at home—and a sign does say "Dress Informal." Contact

Flamingo Lodge
P.O. Box 428
Flamingo, FL 33090-0428
(800) 600-3813

Campgrounds

The National Park Service operates campgrounds at Long Pine Key, Flamingo, and Chekika. All charge fees in peak season and do not accept reservations. For more information, contact the park.

Maps

"Pinelands Trails of the Long Pine Key Area," a free map available at the park's visitor centers, is suitable for this walk.

Fees

Admission to the park is $5 per car.

Points of Interest

The 0.3-mile Anhinga Trail starts at the Royal Palm Visitor Center near Gumbo Limbo Trail. It is the most famous trail in the park and perhaps in the entire national park system. The reason is the wildlife that can be seen along it.

Largemouth bass, tilapias, and gars hang in the current beneath the boardwalk; gators sun themselves on islands; egrets and herons stalk their prey in the shallows; and anhingas and cormorants chase fish beneath the waters of the slough.

Wildlife gathers here because the "River of Grass" dries out in fall and winter, and the animals collect in or near the water that remains. The boardwalk of Anhinga Trail loops out into the sawgrass marsh and crosses Taylor Slough, a creek that stays wet even in the driest years. Sometimes, the animals are so concentrated that they adjust to the crowds of people and behave more like zoo animals than wild creatures in a national park, much·to the delight of tourists.

For some visitors to Everglades National Park, Anhinga Trail is the only trail they have heard of and the only one they want to walk. For many, it is the only direct contact they have with the flora and fauna of this great park. That's too bad, because it gives a misleading impression. As a visit to the remoter areas—Cape Sable, for example, or Ten Thousand Islands—will show, most of the park is truly wild, and this trail is merely the rule-proving exception.

Nonetheless, every visitor to the Everglades should walk Anhinga Trail, if only to see the abundance nature can produce in one place if it has a mind to. It's like watching a nature program on television, and though a few wilderness purists disdain the trail, I wouldn't miss it for the world; for me, every visit to the Everglades starts with a walk on Anhinga Trail.

A note of caution: in the wet season and during wet spells in the dry season, the wildlife of Taylor Slough disperses and the trail reverts to ordinary. Strangely, this is my favorite time on the Anhinga. There is still plenty of wildlife, but you have to work a little harder to find it.

Additional Reading

The Age of Missing Information by Bill McKibben, Random House, New York, 1992.

Dragonflies of the Florida Peninsula, Bermuda and the Bahamas by Sidney W. Dunkle, Scientific Publishers, Gainesville, 1989.

The Everglades Handbook by Thomas E. Lodge, St. Lucie Press, Delray Beach, 1994.

The Everglades: River of Grass by Marjory Stoneman Douglas, Mockingbird Books, St. Simons Island, Georgia, 1974. This reprint of Douglas's 1947 classic includes an afterword added by the author.

Exploring Wild South Florida by Susan D. Jewell, Pineapple Press, Sarasota, 1993.

"The Imaginary Everglades" by Joy Williams, *Outside* 19, January 1994, 38–43 and 90–95.

Land from the Sea: The Geologic Story of South Florida by John Edward Hoffmeister, University of Miami Press, Coral Gables, 1974.

Man in the Everglades by Charlton W. Tebeau, University of Miami Press, Coral Gables, 1968.

The Native Trees of Florida by Erdman West and Lillian Arnold, University of Florida Press, Gainesville, 1956.

The Trees of South Florida, volume 1, by Frank C. Craighead, Sr., University of Miami Press, Coral Gables, 1971.

Adventures in Engineering

Marathon to Pigeon Key via the Old Seven-Mile Bridge
The Middle Keys

The parking area for the old Seven-Mile Bridge is off U.S. I at Marathon, on Knight's Key, just beyond mile marker 47. It is the last turn before the new Seven-Mile Bridge, and if you miss it, the next land you will encounter (and the next place to turn around) is Little Duck Key, at mile marker 40.

From the parking lot, it is a straight shot down the old Seven-Mile Bridge to Pigeon Key. The five-acre island is crisscrossed by paths that lead to historic structures, most of which were associated with the construction of the Overseas Railroad in the early part of this century. Return to the parking area by the same route.

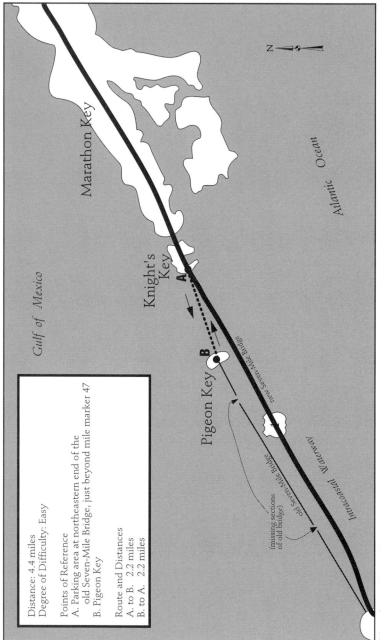

Distance: 4.4 miles
Degree of Difficulty: Easy

Points of Reference
A. Parking area at northeastern end of the
    old Seven-Mile Bridge, just beyond mile marker 47
B. Pigeon Key

Route and Distances
A. to B.   2.2 miles
B. to A.   2.2 miles

Gulf of Mexico

Marathon Key

Knight's
Key

A

B

Pigeon Key

(missing sections
of old bridge)

old Seven-Mile Bridge

new Seven-Mile Bridge

Intracoastal Waterway

Atlantic
Ocean

N

Marathon to Pigeon Key
The Middle Keys

Our first trip to the Keys was in 1966. We rolled out of South Carolina with two kids and a pink plastic diaper pail in the rear seat, pulling a dinged-up rental trailer behind an ancient car completely unsuited for the task. I drove while Diane kept peace in the back. The next day, we pulled into a campsite at John Pennekamp State Park on Key Largo. After snorkeling for a couple of days, we dropped off the kids with some friends who were also staying at the campground and took off for Key West.

Like most first-time visitors to the Keys, we were stunned by what we saw: long, narrow bridges that passed over glowing blue-green waters, waters of a color never seen in South Carolina; brilliant sunshine that filled an endless horizon; and an intermittent strip of bait shops, tiny restaurants, and funky motels lining U.S. 1.

By the time we reached the Seven-Mile Bridge, we were satiated with scenery, but we had one more sight to *ooh* and *ah* over. It appeared as a green oasis beneath the bridge, a picture-perfect postage-stamp-sized tropical island with old wooden houses shaded by coconut palms and bordered on every side by those incredible turquoise waters. The ramp from the bridge to the island was blocked by a gate, so we settled for a black-and-white snapshot taken from a moving car. It wasn't much of a picture, but to us it represented the essence of the tropics. We found out later that the island beneath the bridge was Pigeon Key, and even after dozens of trips to the Keys, that old photograph still conjures up the dreamy day when we saw them for the first time.

Much of what we saw that day no longer exists. The Keys of today resemble the Keys of 1966 in the way that Miami resembles Fernandina Beach. Development is rampant along U.S. 1, tawdrier than ever and no longer intermittent. Wide, soaring spans have replaced the old, low bridges. During the changes, though, Pigeon Key remained a constant, a quaint reminder of simpler days.

When the new Seven-Mile Bridge opened in 1982, the old bridge was closed to automobiles, and it became possible to walk to Pigeon Key. I went several times to get a closer look, but the island, which served as a marine biology center for the University of Miami, remained closed to visitors until 1993, when Monroe County leased it to the Pigeon Key Foundation, which opened it to the public. The walk to Pigeon Key imparts a sense of the natural environment that surrounds this chain of fossilized-coral islands—the birds, the fish, the sea, the seemingly limitless horizon—while the island itself tells another story, a tale of a great adventure in engineering.

I start down the old bridge on a warm, sunny January morning with the wind in my face. In just a few steps, I am over the water. Cormorants perch on the massive concrete pilings that support the new Seven-Mile Bridge. The two bridges angle away from one another, and the rumble of traffic on the new bridge begins to fade as I walk.

To the south is the Atlantic Ocean, to the north the Gulf of Mexico. The two meet about thirty feet below the asphalt surface of the bridge. Stormy weather can make these seas chalky and opaque, but they are clear and cerulean blue today. Gulls rest on sand bars in the Gulf, and pelicans sail down the bridge toward me at alarming speeds. A dozen or so fishermen line the bridge. One of them hooks a small jack and hoists it over the waist-high guardrail. The unusual shape of the stanchions supporting the rail reminds me that this is a bridge with a history.

The original Seven-Mile Bridge was built for a railroad, the Key West Extension of the Florida East Coast Railway. The idea for a railroad from Miami to Key West was Henry Flagler's. Flagler, who made his money in Standard Oil with John D. Rockefeller, owned the Florida East Coast Railway, and his plan was to develop Key West as a deepwater port for trade with Latin American countries, especially Cuba, only ninety miles offshore. Flagler decided to take his railroad to Key West in 1904, and long before the tracks were completed, wags were calling the project "Flagler's Folly."

Establishing the first land route to Key West was a gigantic undertaking. Ralph D. Paine, writing about it in the February 1908 issue of *Everybody's Magazine*, describes the terrain the tracks had to cross:

> This chain of islets swings off from the Everglades of the mainland to stretch down into the Atlantic and the Gulf as far as Key West. [Though the railroad stopped at Key West, the Keys actually extend to the Dry Tortugas.] Worthless, chaotic

fragments of coral reef, limestone, and mangrove swamp, most of them are submerged by high tides and have been aptly called the sweepings and debris which the Creator hurled out to sea after He had finished shaping the Florida peninsula.

Flagler assigned the job of taking his railroad across the Creator's "sweepings and debris" to Joseph C. Meredith, an experienced engineer who had just finished a major construction project in Mexico. For the young engineer, it was the challenge of a lifetime, and he accepted the job eagerly. He died five years later, in 1909, probably from overwork. His assistant William J. Krome took over and finished the job. With Flagler and Krome aboard, the first train from Miami pulled into Key West on January 22, 1912.

It cost Flagler an estimated twenty-eight million dollars to extend the tracks to Key West. Several hundred workers—no one knows exactly how many—and one hard-driving chief engineer lost their lives during the project. Most of the workers died during the three hurricanes that struck the Keys in the eight years it took to lay the tracks. Most of the money, though, was spent building bridges. The longest of these and the most expensive, save one, was the bridge I am walking on—"the Great One," the Seven-Mile Bridge. (Bahia Honda, though shorter than the Seven-Mile Bridge, was the most difficult and most expensive bridge to build because the water it spanned was deeper, the bottom less stable, and the current swifter.)

At the beginning of my walk, Pigeon Key was only a dim green dot in the distance, but after a mile or so, I can see it more clearly, shady and cool beside the bridge. The fronds of the coconut palms on the island flutter in the breeze. Anchored powerboats and the white corks of crab pots bob in the Gulf. There is a light chop on the water beneath the bridge, and ballyhoos lurk just below the surface. Occasionally, shadows of larger fish appear beneath them, and the ballyhoos scatter like mercury poured on a flat surface.

Farther on, dark patches of turtle and manatee grass wave gently in the current. White trails zigzag through the green grass. The trails are prop scars left by boats that careless skippers have plowed through the shallow waters, ripping up grass and disturbing the bottom. Although the waters surrounding the Keys appear the same from year to year to motorists zipping down U.S. 1, they are actually part of a deteriorating ecosystem that starts far north of here in Lake Okeechobee. The ecosystem is troubled because of the growth of population and agriculture in southern Florida in the last half-century.

The Everglades lie almost directly north of Pigeon Key. Fresh water from Lake Okeechobee used to flow freely through the Everglades into Florida Bay. Now, thanks to another vast engineering project, this one by the Corps of Engineers, most of the water is diverted into a network of man-made canals. The canals were dug for flood and mosquito control and to drain the marshes. The used-to-be marshes were then converted into huge fields of tomatoes and sugarcane and houses. Water in the canals is drawn off to irrigate the farms and to slake the thirsts of housing developments and strip malls.

Many (but not all) scientists believe that the dwindling flow of fresh water from the Everglades increased the salinity of Florida Bay, and that much of the water that does reach the bay is agricultural runoff, polluted with dissolved fertilizers and pesticides.

The combination of higher salinity and pollution killed much of the bay's sea grasses. Fueled by rotting grass and nutrients in the runoff, huge patches of pea-green algae began to bloom in Florida Bay. The blooms are shadows of death, cutting off sunlight to the sponges and other marine life at the bottom of the bay and eventually killing them. Blooms have yet to form this far south, but Carl Hiaasen, a novelist who spends a lot of time in the Keys, has reported seeing them at Lignum Vitae Key, only thirty-five miles northeast of here.

The water beneath the bridge becomes shallower. Soon, I am gazing down on Pigeon Key. The gate is open, and after a thirty-year wait, I stroll down the ramp to the island. It is just as I imagined it for all those years: a pocket paradise sitting quietly under the old Seven-Mile Bridge. The grounds are grassy, bordered by mangroves and shaded by palms and hardwoods and Australian pines. Well-tended paths and sidewalks crisscross the island and lead to small wooden buildings. Most of them are closed, but neat white signs identify each one: "Section Gang's Quarters, Main Dining Hall, 1909," "Bridge Foreman's House, Small Guest House, 1916," and so forth. Except for a tiny white bungalow called "Honeymoon Cottage, 1950?" that a brochure explains might have been built for a movie set, the newest building on Pigeon Key is the "Assistant Paint Foreman's House, 1920."

No one knows if Pigeon Key was ever inhabited before the railroad came, nor is there any record of what it looked like before it was transformed into a bustling construction camp for the Overseas Railroad. For a short time, though, life on the island was well documented.

The camp was established in 1908. According to historian Irving Eyster, the original buildings were a dock, a warehouse, four bunkhouses, and a foreman's house. As more laborers poured onto the tiny island, tents were set up to accommodate them. Many of the workers were hobos brought in from New York City, and they named the lanes between tent rows for the streets they knew: Broadway, Fifth Avenue, and Thirty-second Street.

What the 'bos thought of Pigeon Key was not recorded. Although they must have appreciated the weather, the facilities were primitive. Water from cypress holding tanks was piped into some of the houses, but there wasn't a bathroom on the island. Toilets and showers were built over the water.

After the railroad was completed, Pigeon Key served as a maintenance camp for the Florida East Coast Railway. It had a small but permanent population and a tiny schoolhouse. It was a beautiful spot even then, and the train from Miami would sometimes stop so passengers could photograph the idyllic island.

Life on Pigeon Key changed forever on Labor Day morning, September 2, 1935, when the big one hit. It is still called the worst hurricane to ever slam the Keys. The eye passed over the Matecumbe Keys thirty miles northeast of Pigeon Key. Winds of two hundred miles per hour whipped up a twenty-foot storm surge that wiped the Matecumbes clean. Over five hundred people and one railroad died in the storm.

The hurricane flooded Pigeon Key. Residents blocked their doors and windows with mattresses and furniture against the rising water. Surprisingly, no lives were lost. Even more surprisingly, the Seven-Mile Bridge survived the hurricane almost unscathed. But the Florida East Coast Railway, which lost some workers and many miles of track, was finished in the Keys. With Flagler long in his grave, the dispirited company threw in the towel and sold its land and bridges there to the state of Florida for $640,000. The government later appraised the properties at $27,000,000. The hurricane-damaged tracks were never repaired, and the last train from Key West was barged back to Miami.

Nothing on Pigeon Key suggests the despair the hurricane must have produced. It was the middle of the Great Depression, and though the residents and their spick-and-span houses survived, their reason for being was gone. No more trains would stop to allow passengers to photograph the island. Pigeon Key, like the rest of the middle and lower Keys, was cut off again from the mainland.

I wander down to the ocean side of the island. The sharp scent of the sea is strong. An offshore breeze has blown piles of Portuguese men-of-war into low concrete enclosures that were built for a saltwater swimming pool and later used as boat docks. Their purple-tinged floats hide deadly stinging tentacles. Palm trees rattle in the wind, and a kestrel lights in one of the Australian pines. The rest of Pigeon Key's story—the blurry chapters after 1935— can best be found in the steel and concrete that loom over the island, so I follow the ramp back up to the old bridge.

The warm sun is a welcome change from the shade of the island, and with the wind behind me, the walking is easy and fast. About halfway back, I stop to examine the peculiar stanchions I noticed earlier. Each one is made from a section of steel rail cut from the tracks that once crossed the bridge.

After the hurricane, the government decided to reengineer the railway roadbed and convert it into a road for automobiles. The Overseas Railroad became the Overseas Highway, and later U.S.

1. The roadbed of the Seven-Mile Bridge was widened from fourteen to twenty-two feet to accommodate cars, as were all the other bridges except Bahia Honda. There, the automobile road was laid on top of the bridge's steel superstructure, giving early tourists great views and a heart-stopping ride. (A more conventional and far less exciting four-lane bridge has since replaced it.)

The new road opened in 1938. Tolls of one dollar per car were levied at Lower Matecumbe and Big Pine Keys. Pigeon Key became the headquarters for the Bridge and Toll District. An entrepreneur later added a short-lived fishing camp complete with bar and restaurant. The toll booths closed in 1954, and Pigeon Key languished until the University of Miami leased it in the 1960s.

Less than twenty years later, the new Seven-Mile Bridge opened for traffic. The new bridge bypassed Pigeon Key entirely. After the university moved out, the island, which had once housed four hundred railroad workers, was deserted. Today, it is a relic, a piece of history, a place to relive Flagler's Folly and reminisce about a railroad that was once called "the Eighth Wonder of the World" and that was certainly one of the great engineering feats of the twentieth century.

The sun is now directly overhead. Near the end of the bridge, rays and small barracudas swim in the shallow water and gulls sail overhead. Less than a hundred miles from here, another great reengineering project is being contemplated, one that makes turning railway bridges into a highway seem piddling. The Department of the Interior, which manages Everglades National Park, wants the Corps of Engineers to replumb the Everglades. It wants them to undertake an immense project to fix the wrongs caused by the Corps' original canal building and draining, a project that rivaled Flagler's both in magnitude and—if judged by its impact on the Everglades—in folly. The idea is to close many of the canals and reduce the drawdown of water, to reestablish the slow, even flow of fresh water from Lake Okeechobee and re-create the "River of Grass."

Whether the political will exists to actually proceed with such an undertaking is questionable, even if the billions of dollars required for it could be found. But if we could find the money and the will, I suspect the engineers would find a way to do the job. After all, the bridge I just walked across was built over eighty years ago, and it has withstood numerous hurricanes, nature's deadliest punches, with scarcely a scratch. The people who would redo the Everglades, the ones who would actually plan and carry out the work, are the spiritual descendants of the engineers who built this bridge, of Meredith and Krome and the others. Although many people are doubtful about turning the Corps of Engineers loose in the Everglades again, I hope it gets a crack at the job. Engineers didn't create the crowding and environmental problems that afflict the Keys and the Everglades. It's the tasks we set for them and the way we used what they built that caused those problems. Engineers aren't the enemy. We are.

BEFORE YOU GO

For More Information
    Pigeon Key Foundation
    P.O. Box 500130
    Marathon, FL 33050
    (305) 289-0025

Accommodations
    Numerous motels and rental condominiums are available in
Marathon, just north of the Seven-Mile Bridge. Contact
    Greater Marathon Chamber of Commerce
    12222 Overseas Highway
    Marathon, FL 33050
    (800) 842-9580

Campgrounds
    Camping is not permitted on Pigeon Key, but there are several
privately owned campgrounds in the Marathon area. The nearest
public campground is Bahia Honda State Park, 10 miles southwest of Marathon. For information, contact

    Bahia Honda State Park
    Route 1, Box 782
    Big Pine Key, FL 33043
    (305) 872-2353

Maps

A map is not needed; just walk south on the old Seven-Mile Bridge and get off at Pigeon Key.

Fees

Admission to Pigeon Key is $2 if you walk, jog, skate, or bicycle to the island. For others, the Pigeon Key Foundation runs a tram from its office on Knight's Key to Pigeon Key from 9 A.M. to 5 P.M. Tuesday through Sunday. The tram costs $4, which includes the admission fee to Pigeon Key.

Additional Reading

"The Everglades: Dying for Help" by Alan Mairson, *National Geographic* 185, April 1994, 2–35.

The Florida Keys: A History and Guide by Joy Williams, Random House, New York. This excellent guide to the Keys was originally published in 1987. I used the 1990–91 edition.

"The Imaginary Everglades" by Joy Williams, *Outside* 19, January 1994, 38–43 and 90–95.

"Last of the Falling Tide" by Carl Hiaasen, in *Heart of the Land: Essays on Last Great Places*, Pantheon Books, New York, 1994.

"Over the Florida Keys by Rail" by Ralph D. Paine, *Everybody's Magazine* 18, February 1908.

Pigeon Key by Irving R. Eyster. This brochure, published by the Pigeon Key Foundation, is a transcript of Eyster's March 28, 1994, speech on the history of Pigeon Key.

The Railroad That Died at Sea by Pat Parks, Stephen Green Press, Brattleboro, Vermont, 1968.

Birds, Bromeliads, and Field Naturalists

Boardwalk Trail
Corkscrew Swamp Sanctuary

Corkscrew Swamp is an 11,000-acre National Audubon Society sanctuary. It is located near the western edge of Big Cypress National Preserve, in the middle of the triangle formed by Naples, Fort Myers, and Immokalee. From Naples, take I-75 north to C.R. 846 (Exit 17). Proceed east on 846 to a signed entrance to Corkscrew Swamp Sanctuary.

A hard-surfaced path starts at the visitor center and runs a few hundred yards to a boardwalk, which proceeds southwest to a platform overlooking Horseshoe Marsh. Complete the loop by returning on the northern leg of the boardwalk to the trailhead.

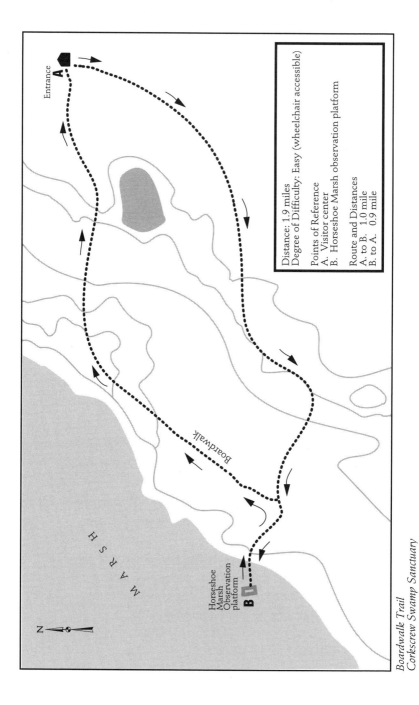

Distance: 1.9 miles
Degree of Difficulty: Easy (wheelchair accessible)

Points of Reference
A. Visitor center
B. Horseshoe Marsh observation platform

Route and Distances
A. to B.   1.0 mile
B. to A.   0.9 mile

Entrance

A

N

MARSH

Boardwalk

Horseshoe
Marsh
Observation
platform

B

Boardwalk Trail
Corkscrew Swamp Sanctuary

Corkscrew Swamp got its name from the Corkscrew River, a winding river that originates in the swamp and resembles—as one might guess—a corkscrew. It was a perfectly good, descriptive name, but it was not grand enough for the developers of nearby Bonita Springs, who renamed it the Imperial River. Since the developers didn't buy the swamp, its name remained unchanged. In fact, much about Corkscrew Swamp has remained unchanged—thanks to the National Audubon Society, which operates a sanctuary here.

The predecessor of the National Audubon Society began posting wardens in Florida as early as 1902 to protect birds from plume hunters. Most of its work was in the Everglades, but the society added a warden in 1912 to oversee the egret rookeries in the great cypress swamps to the north. Thousands of wood storks nested near the egret rookeries, but because their plumage had little value, they didn't need protection. It wasn't until later that the Audubon Society realized the wood storks were in trouble and that the wardens weren't going to be able to help them.

By the early 1950s, the seemingly unlimited cypress forests of "Big Cypress" country were fast disappearing as loggers hacked their way through the swamps. The only large strand of virgin bald cypresses remaining was in Corkscrew Swamp—the nesting site of the wood storks. Lumber companies owned the swamp, and logging was under way when John Hopkinson Baker, the president of the National Audubon Society, began raising money to save Corkscrew.

Baker got involved with the Audubon Society because of his hobby: he was an amateur field naturalist and a dedicated birder. He was a member of the Nuttall Ornithological Club in Cambridge, Massachusetts, and the American Ornithologists' Union. Baker was also a wealthy Harvard-educated investment banker with ties to Wall Street. He became executive director of the National Audubon Society in 1934.

John Baker was a throwback to the era of the white-shoe naturalist, the gentleman birder. But he took his work with the Audubon Society seriously, and the organization flourished under his leadership.

Baker was an effective fund-raiser. In March 1954, he met with representatives of the Lee Tidewater Cypress Company and Collier Enterprises, the companies that owned Corkscrew Swamp. By the end of the year, the National Audubon Society, assisted by other conservation groups, raised $170,000 to buy 2,240 acres in the swamp. Surprisingly, the logging companies were sympathetic to the conservationists' efforts and later chipped in more land at low cost. The result was Corkscrew Swamp Sanctuary, a refuge that contains the country's largest remaining stand of never-cut bald cypresses.

Diane and I arrive at Corkscrew on a perfect winter day. The sun has burned away a morning overcast, leaving a soft blue sky smeared with cirrus clouds. The temperature is in the sixties and rising. The trail that leads into the sanctuary starts near the visitor center at a gazebo surrounded by slash pines. From there, it is a short stroll through pine flatwoods to a boardwalk, which crosses the flat, treeless landscape of a wet prairie. Beyond the prairie looms Corkscrew Swamp, a long, low ridge of shadowy gray cypresses. We follow the boardwalk into the swamp.

This is the dry season, but it has been a wet dry season this year, and black water covers what would normally be dry ground on both sides of the boardwalk. Huge green leaves of arrowhead and smaller shoots of pickerel weed rise from the surface of duck-weed-covered ponds. Sunlight filtering through the leafless cypresses into the lush growth gives the humid air above the water an eerie green glow. Cypress knees and the tall white flowers of arrowhead protrude a foot or two out of the water, and gigantic leather ferns stand well above them. Wax myrtles and pond apples jostle with willows and pop ashes for space in the understory. The scene is one of photosynthesis run amok.

In this struggle for energy, one class of plants developed a unique way of getting sunlight. Its members position themselves below the tops of the cypresses and well above the rough-and-tumble of ground-level competition. Plants of this sort are called epiphytes, or air plants, and they do all the things normal plants do without ever touching the ground.

Epiphytes grow on other plants and on objects such as buildings and telephone wires. They have transcended ordinary plants' need to root in soil, and they are more common than one might think. Mistletoe, for example, is an epiphyte, as are some bromeliads, lichens, orchids, and the ubiquitous Spanish moss, all of which flourish in Corkscrew.

As we follow the boardwalk deeper into the swamp, I begin to sort out some of the more common air plants. We stop to examine a specimen growing fifteen feet above the ground on the trunk of a cypress. It is a *Tilandsia fasciculata*, also known as stiff-leaved wild pine.

T. fasciculata is a bromeliad, a tropical family of plants with spiny leaves and flowers that grow on spikes. Not all bromeliads are epiphytic. The pineapple, for example, is a bromeliad, but it is a conventional plant with roots anchored securely in the ground. With its long, stiff, yellow-green leaves, *T. fasciculata* resembles a pineapple and is sometimes called the "pineapple air plant." Unlike some epiphytes such as mistletoe, *T. fasciculata* and the other bromeliads are not parasitic; they absorb nutrients and water directly from the air or from rainwater that collects in cups formed by their leaves.

Because their nutrients come entirely from the atmosphere, epiphytes are good indicators of air quality. Any trace elements found in them must have been absorbed from the air. Accordingly, some researchers have begun to use Spanish moss to measure air pollution. In these days of tight budgets, replacing a five-thousand-dollar mechanical air sampler with a wad of Spanish moss makes a lot of sense.

The boardwalk next enters an area filled with towering bald cypresses. These are huge trees, twenty-five feet around and well over one hundred feet tall. Cypresses are the oldest trees on the

East Coast, and some of these were already sizable when Columbus set foot in the New World. Resurrection ferns and a startling variety of bromeliads cover every tree. The air has a faint fecund odor. Can you smell chlorophyll? I wonder to myself.

Tiny fish swim among shiny cypress knees in the still, dark water beneath the boardwalk, while woodpeckers hammer away in the distance. A Carolina wren booms out its characteristic *doodlee, doodlee, doodlee,* and two little blue herons stalk fish in the shallow waters of a pond. Above the herons, an anhinga perches in a tree, drying its outstretched wings.

Birds are nearly as plentiful as plants in Corkscrew. This is fitting for a sanctuary managed by an organization named for John James Audubon, the most famous bird man in American history. In 1831 and 1832, Audubon spent six months in Florida. He landed in St. Augustine and traveled down the St. Johns River to Jacksonville. After taking a break in Charleston, South Carolina, he sailed down the coast to Cape Sable and visited Key West and the Dry Tortugas. Audubon never made it to Corkscrew Swamp or even to the west coast of Florida, but as I watch the anhinga sunning itself across the pond, it is his study of this species that comes to mind.

The American anhinga is a large, mostly black water bird with a long neck, a fan-shaped tail, and a sharply pointed beak. Males—like the one I'm watching—have silvery patches on their upper wings. I am only an average birder, unable to distinguish a prairie warbler from a pine warbler at a single glance, so I'm partial to these distinctive birds. They are easy to find and easy to identify, and the species' scientific name, *Anhinga anhinga,* is a piece of cake to remember.

Because anhingas pursue their prey—usually fish—by swimming underwater, they don't need the oily feathers that keep other

birds buoyant. Consequently, they become waterlogged easily and spend a lot of time drying their outspread wings in the sun. Audubon's painting shows an anhinga in just such a pose. The painting emphasizes the anhinga's long, snakelike neck, from which comes its other common name, snakebird.

But it is not Audubon's painting that sticks in my mind when I see the anhinga; it is his introduction to the bird that I found most memorable. In it, Audubon, the quintessential field naturalist, states his disdain for the more academic laboratory- or museum-based scientist. Not much has changed since Audubon wrote the passage; I have heard modern field biologists express almost identical views.

Many writers have described what they have been pleased to call the habits of the Anhinga; nay, some have presumed to offer comments upon them, and to generalize and form theories thereon, or even to inform us gravely and oracularly what they ought to be, when the basis of all their fancies was merely a dried skin and feathers appended. Leaving these ornithologists for the present to amuse themselves in their snug closets, I proceed to detail the real habits of this curious bird, as I have observed and studied them in Nature.

Audubon follows this diatribe with eight pages of his observations of anhingas and includes a sentence that proudly describes how one must "venture through mud and slime up to his very neck to get within rifle shot" of these wary birds. Later, he points out that wading through mud and slime has its own pleasures for a real naturalist: "With what anxiety have I waded toward these birds, to watch their movements, while at the same time I cooled my overheated body, and left behind on the shores myriads of hungry sand-flies, gnats, mosquitoes, and ticks, that had annoyed me for hours!"

I think about wading through the black water of the scum-covered pond in front of me to better observe the anhinga I have been watching. But I'm not overheated, and no sandflies, gnats, mosquitoes, or ticks are bugging me, so I raise my binoculars instead. The anhinga ignores me and never moves a feather. I whisper into my tape recorder, "Anhingas are not particularly wary of field naturalists, as long as they don't disturb them by wading through mud and slime."

The boardwalk ends at a low platform overlooking Horseshoe

Marsh. Saw grass and arrowhead mingle with stunted willows on a treeless plain that is as flat as a southern Florida freeway. I scan the cypresses behind the platform, looking for the huge, messy nests of Corkscrew's most famous birds, but the trees are empty of both nests and wood storks this year.

When we first visited Corkscrew, in the winter of 1982, the trees were full of nesting storks. Huge black-and-white birds with bare, black heads and wingspreads exceeding five feet came and went constantly, bringing fish to squealing chicks or sticks to shore up their coarse nests. Where are they today? The answer lies in the water standing beside the boardwalk. Although wood storks feed in water, there is too much of it this year.

The wood stork, *Mycteria americana*, is a grope feeder. It wades in shallow ponds, keeping its large, partially opened bill in the water. When it feels something alive, it snaps its bill shut and swallows the prey. Usually, this is a fish, but the wood stork's diet also includes frogs, tadpoles, small alligators, snakes, and insects. Grope feeders aren't choosy; whatever they manage to grab, they eat.

Wood storks nest in large colonies during the winter dry season, when fish are concentrated in small, shallow pools. Their prey is easy to catch then, and the surplus feeds their ravenous chicks. High water, though, means tough times for wood storks. Some pools become too deep to wade and others expand in area, giving fish more room to hide from the birds' powerful, groping bills. In a very wet winter like this one, food is so hard to find that the storks must disperse to survive. Under such conditions, they don't nest at all. So Corkscrew Swamp, the largest wood-stork rookery in Florida, is silent and empty of those great birds in this aberrant year.

Of course, there might still be one or two around. I scan the marsh and the trees carefully. I spot a red-shouldered hawk in a tall cypress at the edge of the marsh—but no storks.

We leave Horseshoe Marsh and begin our return on the northern leg of the boardwalk. An occasional royal palm stands among the cypresses, and royal, swamp, and marsh ferns grow lushly among the knees, as do dark green sweet bays. The vegetation is so dense that the boardwalk is cool and shady even though the cypresses are bald this time of year. A red-bellied woodpecker flies overhead, and two pileateds sit high in a cypress. The boardwalk crosses a lake so thick with vegetation that it obscures the surface of the water. This is one of the aptly named lettuce lakes, and it looks more like a lawn than a lake.

The vegetation growing in the lake isn't grass, though, it's water lettuce, *Pistia stratiotes*, a leafy, light green plant that floats on the surface of the water and vaguely resembles iceberg lettuce. Some lakes—this one included—are so thickly packed with the stuff that they appear solid. Eventually, water lettuce will kill this lake, filling it in as dead plants fall to the bottom and turn into partially rotted muck. Today, though, it is very much alive, providing perfect habitat for a trio of alligators sunning themselves on the far shore. With my binoculars, I check the lake for storks but see none.

The boardwalk continues east past tall cypresses decorated with lichens and orchids and tufts of Spanish moss. According to a boardwalk guide I picked up at the visitor center, otters and bobcats and bears still roam Corkscrew Swamp, but the only mammals we have seen today are gray squirrels, which chatter at us from the trees.

After we finish our walk, we meet Phoebe, a tall, thin woman dressed in a spiffy tan uniform. She is an amateur naturalist who spends most of her time in the field as a "boardwalk volunteer," cruising the sanctuary, answering visitors' questions, and observing wildlife. Phoebe knows all about storks. She tells us that high water has stopped them from nesting anywhere in southern Florida this year. In fact, she says, they are hard to find at all. "Look for them in the shallow canals beside the road," she advises.

Phoebe turns out to be not only knowledgeable but a prophetess as well. As we leave the refuge, two wood storks rise from a canal beside the road and fly over our car. I think back to the achievements of John James Audubon and John Baker and mentally chalk up another success for the field naturalists of the world.

BEFORE YOU GO

For More Information

Corkscrew Swamp Sanctuary
375 Sanctuary Road
Naples, FL 33964
(941) 657-3771

Accommodations

Corkscrew Swamp is about equidistant from Naples, Fort Myers, Immokalee, and Bonita Springs.

A variety of accommodations is available in Naples, which is about 35 miles southwest of Corkscrew. Contact

Naples Chamber of Commerce
3620 Tamiami Trail North
Naples, FL 33940
(941) 278-1231

For information on lodging in Fort Myers and Bonita Springs, contact

Lee County Visitor and Convention Bureau
2180 First Street, Suite 100
Fort Myers, FL 33901
(800) 237-6444

For lodging in Immokalee, contact

Immokalee Chamber of Commerce
907 Roberts Avenue
Immokalee, FL 33934
(941) 657-3237

Campgrounds

Camping is not permitted in Corkscrew Swamp Sanctuary. The nearest public campground is at Koreshan State Historic Site, near Estero. For information, contact

Koreshan State Historic Site
P.O. Box 7

Estero, FL 33928
(941) 992-0311

Maps

No map is needed for this walk; however, the booklet *Cork-screw Swamp Sanctuary: A Self-Guided Tour of the Boardwalk*, which contains a useful guide to the numbered stations along the board-walk, has a map on the back. The booklet is free if you return it after your walk.

In 1996, after we took our walk, the National Audubon Soci-ety replaced and rerouted parts of the boardwalk and lengthened it overall. The new boardwalk gives you the option of a longer walk than the one described here, which will allow you to see more of this endlessly fascinating swamp. I look forward to check-ing out this route on our next visit to Corkscrew; I hope you will, too.

Fees

Admission to the boardwalk is $6.50 per adult. College stu-dents and members of the National Audubon Society get in for $5.00. Children under six years old are admitted free.

Additional Reading

The Audubon Ark by Frank Graham, Jr., with Carl W. Buchheister, Alfred A. Knopf, New York, 1990. This is an excellent history of the National Audubon Society. I used this book extensively in digging out the events surrounding the Audubon Society's pur-chase of Corkscrew Swamp.

Audubon in Florida by Kathryn Hall Proby, University of Mi-

ami Press, Coral Gables, 1974. The quotes from Audubon's writings were taken from this book.

"Delicate Balance: Wood Stork" by Janisse Ray, *Florida Wildlife* 49, May–June 1995, 29.

John James Audubon: A Biography by Alexander B. Adams, Capricorn Books, G. P. Putnam's Sons, New York, 1966.

Vascular Epiphytes by David H. Benzig, Cambridge University Press, Cambridge, England, 1990.

CENTRAL

[The sun's] glories appear on the forests, encompassing the
meadows, and gild the top of . . . the exalted Palms, now rustling by
the pressure of the waking breezes.

WILLIAM BARTRAM, 1791

A Varied but Constant Land

Bee Island Loop
Myakka River State Park

At 28,874 acres, Myakka River is Florida's largest state park. It lies 15 miles east of downtown Sarasota (9 miles east of I-75) on S.R. 72.

This walk starts at a signed, locked gate 5 miles from the entrance station, just beyond the parking area for Upper Myakka Lake. An old road leads 0.2 mile from the main road to the trailhead. It is another 0.2 mile to the beginning of the Bee Island loop. Though the loop can be hiked in either direction, I prefer counterclockwise because you finish the walk in the welcome shade of an oak-palm hammock.

The white-blazed loop trail passes through an ever-changing landscape of hammocks, dry prairies, and pine flatwoods. After 5 miles, it intersects the blue-blazed Bee Island Cross Trail. Take the cross trail east for 2 miles. The well-marked path passes the pine flatwoods of Bee Island and an oak-palm hammock with campsites for backpackers, then rejoins the loop trail. The loop trail traverses a vast, dry prairie for several miles, then enters a shady hammock for the final leg back to the trailhead.

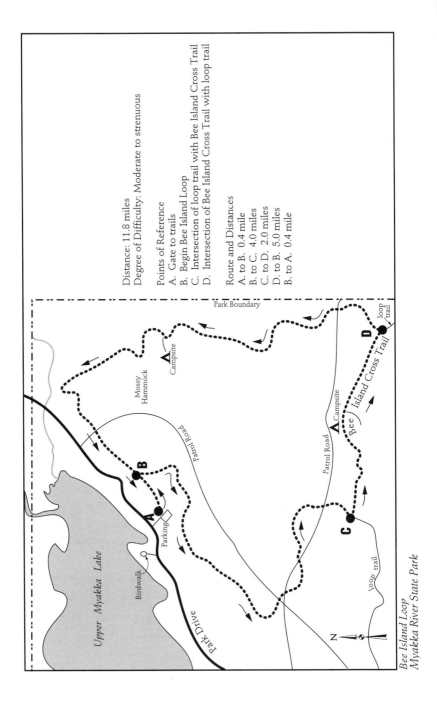

Distance: 11.8 miles
Degree of Difficulty: Moderate to strenuous

Points of Reference
A. Gate to trails
B. Begin Bee Island Loop
C. Intersection of loop trail with Bee Island Cross Trail
D. Intersection of Bee Island Cross Trail with loop trail

Route and Distances
A. to B. 0.4 mile
B. to C. 4.0 miles
C. to D. 2.0 miles
D. to B. 5.0 miles
B. to A. 0.4 mile

Park Boundary

Mossy
Hammock

Campsite

Patrol Road

B

A

Parking

Birdwalk

Upper Myakka Lake

Park Drive

Patrol Road

Campsite

Bee Island Cross Trail

D

loop
trail

C

loop trail

N

Bee Island Loop
Myakka River State Park

Myakka River State Park is a crazy quilt of ecosystems. Prairies, flatwoods, and hammocks are interspersed with
lakes, streams, and wetlands. Slash pines grow here, live oaks there,
and no trees at all over yonder. Pure stands of saw palmettos flourish
along one trail, while broom sedge and other grasses prevail on
another. Water-dependent ospreys nest at Myakka River, but so
do forest-loving warblers and woodpeckers. Otters cavort in streams
while armadillos snuffle through leaf litter on the banks a few
feet away.

A nineteenth-century tourist, F. Trench Townshend, left a written account of the varied landscape. Townshend accepted this
patchwork land as it was and didn't speculate much about how it
got that way. Today, ecologists worry about such things. They believe that small changes in elevation and in the frequency of fires
played important roles in forming the many ecosystems in the
park.

Throughout the region, the water table is close to the surface
because of poorly drained soil, so heavy rainfall produces seasonal
wetlands in the slightest of depressions. Fires are required to maintain the park's extensive flatwoods and prairies. Nature obliges

with lightning strikes, and when nature is not forthcoming, the park service has begun to help out with controlled burns. Hardwood hammocks, on the other hand, form only where fire is excluded, so hammocks are often found downwind of lakes and wetlands.

Three of the park's most important ecosystems meet at an old sand road near Bee Island, the halfway point of this walk. South of the road is an oak-palm hammock embedded in a great swath of pine flatwoods. To the north, a dry prairie stretches to the horizon. The view nicely illustrates the park's diversity.

We start the trail on a cool January morning. It rained last night, and low fog lies over the wet ground. Epiphytes cover the live oaks beside the trail. The resurrection ferns that line the oaks' massive limbs are bright green with moisture; the Spanish moss is dull gray. As we walk, Diane points out other common epiphytes— wild pine, a bromeliad that resembles a tuft of pine needles, and quill leaf, which looks like a pineapple plant.

Lichens decorate the gray trunks of laurel oaks, and an occasional slash pine towers over the hardwoods. The understory is saw palmettos and wax myrtles. This is an easy ecosystem to identify, but just as I say "Mixed hardwood hammock" into my tape recorder, the trail breaks into the open.

Trees become sparse. Ten-foot-tall fetterbushes and saw palmettos, evidence of years of fire suppression, grow along the narrow trail, almost enveloping it. A black vulture perches in a bleached snag, and tree swallows zip across the top of the brush, picking off insects. But by the time I say "Dry prairie" into my tape recorder, my boots begin to stick in the mud.

Water stands in the grass beside the trail. The presence of St.-John's-worts and bachelor's-buttons indicate that we are entering a new ecosystem, a wetland. The path crosses a tiny stream. Another wetlands plant, pickerel weed, grows at the water's edge.

Beyond the stream are signs of an unwelcome visitor. Something has chewed up a sizable patch of damp, black earth. The ground looks as if it has been attacked by a maniac with a rototiller, but the area is crisscrossed with the tracks of the real culprits: feral pigs. The pigs root through the moist soil of wetlands searching for edible roots and in the process damage native plants. It is no surprise to find wild pigs here. Although they are not native to Myakka, they've been around a long time.

Though it has no distinct boundaries, the region east of Sarasota has long been known as Myakka. The name came from a surveyor who in 1843 encountered some Seminole Indians at the mouth of a waterway then called the Asternal River. The surveyor asked them the name of the river. The Indians replied with a word that sounded like *Miarca* to the surveyor, who dutifully recorded it. In later maps, *Miarca* mutated to *Myakka*. Since then, a lot of folks have claimed to know what the name means.

I have a serious hang-up with Indian names. White writers often tell of one-word Indian names that supposedly mean "Land Where the Blue Water Laps the Green Shores" or "Place Where the Tall Mountains Pierce the Sky" or some other nonsense. I vowed years ago never to give the definition of an Indian word unless I found it in a dictionary or was told its meaning by a Native American who spoke the language. Which brings me back to *Myakka*.

Over the years, several writers have presumed to know what *Myakka* means in the Seminole language. In a recent magazine article, one stated flatly that it is a Seminole word meaning "Big Water." But Paula Benshoff, a ranger at Myakka River State Park who is as skeptical about these things as I am, checked it out. She spoke to Steven Bowers, a project coordinator of Indian affairs in Hollywood, Florida. Bowers's parents spoke Creek and Mikasuki, the two languages of the Seminoles. He told Paula that there was no word in either language that sounded like *Myakka* or *Miarca* and that the words therefore have no Seminole meaning.

In any case, the river with the meaningless name drained the region east of Sarasota, and by the middle of the nineteenth century, people were calling the area *Myakka* (often spelled *Miakka*). Almost nothing is known of the Indians who lived in Myakka before Europeans came. Early settlers told of Indian mounds, but these tales have not been documented. In fact, little is known of the earliest settlers themselves. Townshend, one of those intrepid British travelers who roamed the globe in the nineteenth century searching for adventure and sport, offered one of the first written descriptions of the region. He came to Myakka in 1874 with his companion, Edmund A. Mansfield, and this is what he said about the country:

> Having procured, for a consideration of six dollars a day, a waggon [*sic*] and mule team with an intelligent youth to drive and guide us, we started in the middle of February for the Myakka Lakes . . . a part of the country where we were assured large game was abundant, and turkeys so numerous that they could be knocked off the trees by hundreds. We were at the same time warned that we should have to rough it in the severest sense of the term, a warning which turned out perfectly true, and free from exaggeration, which is more than I can say for the account of the turkeys.

When the party reached Myakka, it stayed with a Dr. Huff, whose house was a mile from Upper Myakka Lake, somewhere within the boundaries of today's state park. Townshend described Dr. Huff as a "stock-owner and farmer." And if the number of turkeys in Myakka disappointed the two Englishmen, the abundance of wild hogs got their attention:

> Throughout the Peninsula of Florida, large herds of hogs are raised and roam the forests half wild, finding an independent support on the mast of the oak, the palmetto and other fruit-bearing trees scattered among the pine and hammock lands. As wild hogs also abound, and are in the habit of inducing the tame sows to retire with them into the woods, and there bring up their progeny in a wild state, it becomes necessary to form hunting parties to kill the wild hogs.

We continue through the wetlands, leaving behind the disturbed black earth that was probably plowed up by the descendants of the tough, lean hogs hunted by Townshend over one hundred years ago. The underbrush closes in again. Swamp bays and ferns crowd the muddy path. We cross another, wider stream with a white-sand bottom. Minnows swim in the tannin-stained water, and arrowhead grows exuberantly in the streambed. The muck of the trail preserves perfectly the long-fingered tracks of a raccoon.

Near Bee Island Cross Trail, the country changes again. A dry, sandy expanse of prairie replaces the wetlands. Instead of swamp bays and ferns, knee-high grasses and saw palmettos cover the ground. Two red-shouldered hawks perch on a distant snag.

By now, the morning fog is gone. The sun is bright and hot. An osprey flaps overhead, clutching a still-wriggling fish in its talons. Both osprey and fish look decidedly out of place in this dry, treeless land. The large stand of pines known as Bee Island looms in the distance.

On his trip to Myakka, Townshend noticed that Floridians often referred to the isolated hammocks and stands of pines that break up the prairie as "islands":

> Besides the hammocks and pine land, the interior . . . is for the most part covered with prairie, or "perairer," as the natives call it, consisting of low saw-palmetto and grass, on the latter of which great herds of cattle are pastured; ponds fringed with tall saw-grass are scattered over these prairies, and belts of timber, composed of pine and cabbage palm intersect them, and are called by the natives "islands."

The heart of Bee Island is an oak-palm hammock, which is surrounded by pine flatwoods. We have lunch sitting on a log in the welcome shade of a live oak dripping with Spanish moss. Carolina wrens call insistently in the forest, and the fronds of cabbage palms clatter in the breeze. Armadillos nose through the soft soil, searching for insects.

After lunch, we leave the hammock and continue west through pine flatwoods. Most of the trees are longleaf pines, and every trunk is scorched from the fires that have raced through the underbrush beneath them. The fires burn back the brush and thin the young pines, keeping the understory low and the trees scattered. (See the chapter entitled "A Forest Redux" for a more complete account of the effects of fire on longleaf-pine habitats.) The result is an open, aesthetically pleasing landscape with an odor that the manufacturers of pine-scented car fresheners have never been able to duplicate.

The openness of the pine flatwoods was also noticed by Townshend, who appreciated it for more utilitarian reasons:

> In the Northern forests no man on horseback could possibly force his way through without free use of the axe, owing to the accumulation of fallen timber and the fact of the trees growing so close together. . . . But in Florida, except in the swamps and hammocks, the forests are so open that a horseman could penetrate from one end of the country to another.

A gator bellows from an unseen pond, a stentorian roar that stops us in our tracks. We wait for the gator to continue, but all is quiet, so we walk on. Tiny olive-colored warblers flit through the pines. They are pine warblers, birds that are rarely found far from pine trees and that invariably choose to nest in them.

The trail leaves the shady island of pines and enters another prairie. The prairie we passed earlier was a postage stamp compared to this one. This is the real thing, a vast, treeless expanse of dry prairie, the most distinctive and most prevalent ecosystem in the park.

We start across it. The temperature is in the low seventies, but the afternoon sun makes it feel hotter, and beads of sweat roll down my face and sting my eyes. The only shade comes from the fleeting shadows of a pair of turkey vultures floating ominously overhead.

Waist-high scrub oaks, fetterbushes, and blueberries grow beside the sandy trail, and clumps of shiny black berries cling to low-lying gallberry bushes. But the most common plant by far is the ubiquitous saw palmetto, *Serenoa repens*.

Throughout Florida, thickets of saw palmettos occur as understory in hammocks and pine flatwoods. But out here on the open prairie, they dominate. Some of the saw palmettos have short, sizable trunks. A few are upright, but most lie flat against the ground. Every trunk, vertical or prostrate, is blackened by fire.

The common name for the saw palmetto comes from its rasp-edged leaf stalks. And though I love the wide-open spaces of this prairie and enjoy sorting out the plants in it, I wouldn't want to walk here unless I had a decent trail to follow. Townshend, who crossed here 120 years earlier, didn't have a trail, and his reaction to the prairie was considerably less charitable than mine: "I know few places more unpleasant to travel over than these Florida prairies, where the head and body are scorched by the sun, and legs are torn by the sharp teeth of the saw-palmetto."

After walking a mile or so, we are hotter and thirstier than ever. Diane is tired of listening to me try to identify every stalk of grass we pass. As far as she's concerned, the romance of the prairie is wearing thin. She hums a song that sounds like "Cool Water." A clump of trees on the horizon grows larger. At 2:43 P.M., I make a note, "Passing the first tree we've seen in an hour." Minutes later, the trail enters a forest of live oaks and cabbage palms. We have reached the last major ecosystem we'll encounter on this walk: the oak-palm hammock.

The hammock is shady and cool, with tall cabbage palms and huge, epiphyte-covered live oaks. It is also filled with birds, which, except for buzzards, were hard to spot on the prairie. The bird list I picked up this morning says that wild turkeys are common in the park, so I keep an eye out for them. I spot two red-headed woodpeckers, bright mosaics of black and white and red. A little farther along is a flock of thirty or so robins. Grackles, wrens, mockingbirds, cardinals, and crows hop about in the oaks croaking and singing. Avian life of all sorts abounds—except wild turkeys.

Nonetheless, compared to the still, sun-baked prairie, hammocks are lively places. Townshend noticed the same thing when he traveled through a hammock over a century ago:

> [We] found ourselves in a dense jungle of tall cabbage-palm, oak, and willow, where the fresh green leaves of the wild vine and other creepers formed a delicious roof above our heads, sheltering us from the burning sun. A legion of song birds, the red bird and the sweet-toned mocking-bird conspicuous among them, sent forth their music from every tree.

Almost as numerous as the birds are armadillos, which weren't here when Townshend visited Myakka. These days, they are everywhere, and they ignore us so completely that I decide to test one's nerve. I close in on it as it plods along, nose to the ground. It pays no attention. I touch its tough, leathery armor. No response. Finally, I grab its tail. The armadillo digs its powerful claws into the ground and leaps forward, freeing itself. It then goes back to probing the earth. Except for a hungry black bear with its nose in my picnic cooler, one extraordinarily pugnacious cottonmouth, and an alligator or two, I have never encountered a wild animal with less fear of humans than this armadillo.

Armadillos evolved in South America, where twenty species still survive. Only one, the nine-banded armadillo (*Dasypus novemcinctus*), has made it to North America. With rabbitlike ears, a piglike snout, a tortoiselike carapace, and the long, sensitive tongue of an anteater, armadillos look as if they were designed by a politician trying to please everybody. They eat insects and other invertebrates, which they find by sniffing through leaf litter. They weigh about ten pounds and have one of the smallest brains of any North American mammal.

Nine-banded armadillos entered this country around 1850, crossing the Rio

Grande and spreading through the Southwest. The Myakka population may be descended from animals that escaped from a zoo in Cocoa, Florida, in the 1920s. Though armadillos were latecomers to the United States, the country seems to suit them. According to one estimate, thirty to fifty million of them now live here. How did such tiny-brained animals manage to adapt so well to a new environment? Well, as modern evolutionary biologists are so fond of telling us, evolution is unplanned, and intelligence is only one of many characteristics that help organisms survive and procreate.

The trail takes us deeper into the shadowy hammock. The black dirt of the path becomes soggier. Unlike the prairie and the pine flatwoods (and some hammocks), this hammock has no fire scars. Its dampness and the direction of the prevailing winds have protected it. In here, the open prairie seems like a sun-blasted daydream.

A stream rises beside the trail. Tea-colored water flows over a white-sand bottom. The limbs of some of the live oaks near the stream are so massive that they rest on the ground. Squirrels chatter at us as we pass, and armadillos plow through the forest duff beside the creek. A head appears in the middle of the stream, moving fast enough to leave a wake. It turns toward the far shore, and a sleek brown otter scrambles up a muddy bank, then stops and peers inquisitively at us.

Some scientists would consider my use of the word *inquisitively* as anthropomorphic, but every otter I've seen in the wild has been unmistakably curious about humans. They stop whatever they're doing, watch you with bright brown eyes that show no hint of belligerence or fear, then disappear. This animal is no exception. After a moment, it bounds down the steep bank, as lithe as a fur-covered Slinky, and vanishes into the stream.

Near the end of the walk, we spot the remains of three vats, artifacts of a cattle ranch that once flourished here. Nobody knows exactly when cattle were introduced to southwestern Florida, but ranching was already important when Townshend visited Tampa in 1874. "There are about six hundred inhabitants chiefly engaged in the cattle trade," he wrote, "the export to Cuba of both cattle and hogs being a large and profitable business."

Townshend mentioned that cattle roamed Myakka, but ranching back then was a haphazard, catch-as-catch-can business. The situation began to change thirty-six years later when Mrs. Potter Palmer, a well-heeled Chicago widow, bought much of Myakka. Mrs. Palmer brought newfangled ways to the business: she fenced her land; she imported new breeds of cattle that were better able to withstand the Florida heat; and she began dipping her stock in vats to rid the cows of the ticks that plagued them.

After Mrs. Palmer's death in 1918, her heirs managed the ranch until the 1920s, when they abandoned it. The land sat idle until 1934, when the Civilian Conservation Corps established a camp on the Myakka River. In 1941, Mrs. Palmer's ranch became part of the new Myakka River State Park.

Considering its extensive use by humans, the Myakka country of today is remarkably similar to what Townshend observed when he trekked in from Tampa. Of course, changes have occurred: the cows are gone, the armadillos have come, and well-maintained foot trails have replaced Townshend's rough tracks. But the ecosystems he described—the prairies, hammocks, pinelands, and wetlands—still exist essentially unchanged. The songbirds, the wild hogs, and the otters are still here, too. And there's one more constant: wild turkeys are still scarcer than advertised.

BEFORE YOU GO

For More Information
Myakka River State Park
13207 State Road 72
Sarasota, FL 34241-9542
(941) 361-6511

Accommodations
Sarasota is convenient to the park. It has hotels and motels to suit every pocketbook. Contact

Sarasota Convention and Visitors Bureau
655 North Tamiami Trail
Sarasota, FL 34236
(800) 522-9799

Campgrounds
The park has two family campgrounds. Big Flats has 52 sites, and Old Prairie has 24. The park also rents five air-conditioned log cabins near Old Prairie Campground; these cabins were built by the Civilian Conservation Corps in the 1930s.

Six primitive campgrounds are scattered along the park's hiking trails to accommodate backpackers. Each one has a well and a hand pump. The wells occasionally run dry, and even when water is available, the park service advises hikers to purify it before drinking.

Maps

The trail map in the brochure *Backpacking* is adequate for this walk. The map accurately depicts the trails, but it does not show the many sand roads that crisscross the park. If you stick to the hiking trails, you'll be fine. If you try to take a shortcut on a road (as we did), you may get lost (as we did).

The park is developing a new and better map, which should be available in 1997.

Fees

The park charges a $3.25 entrance fee per car. A fee schedule for campsites and cabins is available.

Points of Interest

The park has a 35-mile network of well-marked trails. The trails form four connected loops, the innermost of which is the Bee Island loop. Because of their distance from the trailhead, the outer loops are best suited for backpacking.

Additional Reading

Afoot in the South: Walks in the Natural Areas of North Carolina by Phillip Manning, John F. Blair, Publisher, Winston-Salem, North Carolina, 1993.

"The Armadillo Is Not Just Another Pretty Face" by Bil Gilbert, *Smithsonian* 26, October 1995, 142–51. This excellent article by one of the country's premier magazine writers tells the armadillo's story in detail.

"The Dry Prairie and Its Birds" by Michael F. Delany, *Florida Wildlife* 49, September–October 1995, 12–14.

"A History of Myakka" by Paula Benshoff. I drew heavily on this manuscript, which is available at the park office. I am indebted to Benshoff for allowing me to see her work prior to its publication.

"Vascular Flora of Myakka River State Park, Sarasota and Manatee Counties, Florida" by Jean M. Huffman. This unpublished manuscript is available at the park office.

Wild Life in Florida with a Visit to Cuba by F. Trench Townshend, Hurst and Blackett, Publishers, London, 1875.

Climbing Elton's Pyramid

Buster Island Loop
Lake Kissimmee State Park

Three lakes—Kissimmee, Rosalie, and Tiger—ring the 5,030-acre Lake Kissimmee State Park, which lies 19 miles east of the town of Lake Wales. From Lake Wales, take U.S. 60 east for 9 miles to Boy Scout Road. Proceed north on Boy Scout Road for 4 miles, then take a right on Camp Mack Road. The park entrance is 6 miles from the intersection of Boy Scout and Camp Mack Roads. The entrance road ends at a parking lot, where the trail begins.

From the parking lot, an access trail leads 0.5 mile across Rosalie Drain and past Cow Camp (a re-creation of an 1876 cattle ranch) to a sign where the Buster Island loop starts. At the sign, bear right to walk the loop counterclockwise. Return to the parking lot by the same access trail.

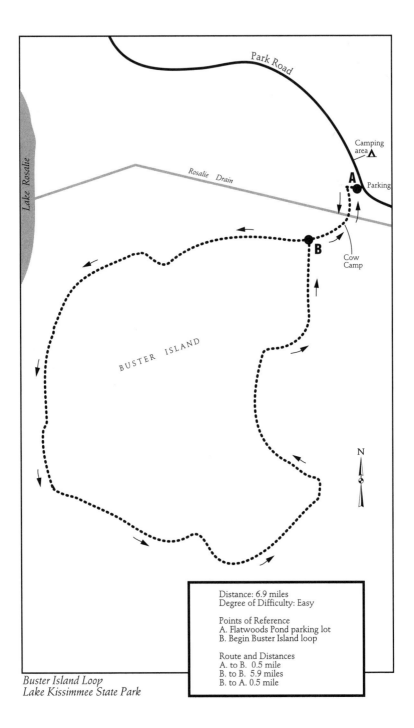

Park Road

Lake Rosalie

Camping area △

Rosalie Drain

A Parking

Cow Camp

B

BUSTER ISLAND

N

Distance: 6.9 miles
Degree of Difficulty: Easy

Points of Reference
A. Flatwoods Pond parking lot
B. Begin Buster Island loop

Route and Distances
A. to B. 0.5 mile
B. to B. 5.9 miles
B. to A. 0.5 mile

Buster Island Loop
Lake Kissimmee State Park

It was one of those balmy winter evenings you sometimes get in Orlando. Glasses clinked and guests circulated around the pool. Our host was an old friend, Milt Gillespie. On noticing that I wasn't circulating properly, he introduced me to another guest, a stunning woman with long silver hair.

"Milt tells me you write books. Are you working on one now?" she asked.

"Yes," I replied. "It's about one-day walks in the ecosystems of Florida."

"That's wonderful. Does Florida have a lot of them?"

"Ecosystems? Oh, yes. Lots."

"How do you tell them apart?" she asked politely.

I began with hardwood hammocks, with their huge live oaks and Spanish moss. When I moved on to the wire grass of the high-pine ecosystem, her eyes began to wander. By the time I got around to explaining the differences between Florida scrub and pine flatwoods—for example, how *Ceratiola ericoides* is almost never found in flatwoods and *Persea borbonia* is absent from scrub—they were glazed over. I was barely into the shrubs of the highland marshes before she excused herself, staggered to the bar, demanded a double martini—and avoided me for the rest of the night.

Detailed descriptions of ecosystems have that effect on people. Lists of the flora that define an ecosystem bore them. However, mention your encounter with a bald eagle or the time you saw four white-tailed deer frozen like hood ornaments in the sun-dappled woods and you will get a more enthusiastic response. Most of us relate better to animals than to plants. Birders are a dime a dozen, but tree watchers are hard to find.

Fortunately, there is a less precise but more interesting way to identify ecosystems. The principle was stated by Charles Elton in his groundbreaking 1927 book, *Animal Ecology*: "One of the first things with which an ecologist has to deal is the fact that each different kind of habitat contains a characteristic set of animals." In other words, animals as well as plants can define a habitat.

Ecologists don't ordinarily use animals to describe an ecosystem because plants are less mobile and more numerous. It's easier to find and identify a myrtle oak than it is to spot a scrub jay, though both are found in the scrub ecosystem.

Elton dealt with this phenomenon in his book. He formulated the "Pyramid of Numbers," a theory that predicts the relative populations of animals one might expect to find in an ecosystem. Today, Elton's pyramid, expanded to include plants, is found in every first-year biology textbook. At the base of the pyramid is the vegetation. As the pyramid narrows, one encounters the herbivores and then the carnivores. The point is that it takes a lot of plants to support an herbivore and a lot of herbivores to support a carnivore. Thus, in an ecosystem, plants are common, herbivores less common, and carnivores rare.

Nonetheless, where wildlife is abundant, as it is at Lake Kissimmee State Park, animals can be useful in identifying ecosystems—which is what I have in mind when Diane and I arrive there a few days later.

We start the access trail that leads to the Buster Island loop on a warm January morning. The sky is overcast, and a light breeze inexplicably carries the faint scent of dill. The trail crosses Rosalie Drain—a canal that links Lake Rosalie to Lake Kissimmee—then passes a replica of an 1876 cow camp, which is closed today. Pine flatwoods border huge pastures, and you don't need the cow camp to guess that this land was recently a working cattle ranch. In fact, Lake Kissimmee didn't become a state park until 1977.

The trail enters a sliver of forest filled with live oaks and cabbage palms and saw palmettos, bordered by fields and edged with slash pines. Deer tracks cover the path. Suddenly, the real thing—a doe—bounds across the path not fifty feet in front of us and vanishes into the woods. I stop to glass the woods for the deer. Though the understory is sparse, there is no sign of her. I'm not surprised; I've stumbled on lots of deer in my walks, but I've never been able to spot one in a forest after it's decided to hide. That is one reason deer prefer terrain where field and forest rub against each other. They can hide in the forest and feed in the fields.

Country like this is called "edge habitat," and though white-tailed deer favor it, they also live in the deep woods, albeit in reduced numbers. Elton called animals that can live in an ecosystem but are not confined to it "characteristic" species of that ecosystem. He called those that can exist only in that ecosystem "exclusive" species. Thus, deer are a characteristic species of the edge habitat, while Florida jays—which live only in scrub—are exclusive to that ecosystem.

The trail continues deeper into the oak-palm hammock. Forest-loving warblers flit through the oaks, and armadillos nose through forest duff. A high-pitched squeal stops us in our tracks. After a few moments, we locate its source, a huge pile of sticks in the top of a slash pine near the edge of the hammock. An eaglet peers over the top of the nest.

Circling above the eaglet are a bald eagle and a red-tailed hawk. The eagle doesn't appear to be chasing the hawk, and the hawk doesn't appear to be threatening the eagle's nest. They are simply soaring in wide circles around one another. *What are they doing?* I suspect the eagle is keeping an eye on the hawk in the vicinity of its nest, but many old-time naturalists would disagree. In his *Life Histories of North American Birds of Prey*, Arthur Cleveland Bent stated unequivocally that "the bald eagle is an arrant coward [in defending its nest] . . . squealing, or perching on a distant tree to watch proceedings."

Bald eagles have never received much respect in this country. Benjamin Franklin didn't care for them; he favored the wild turkey for our national bird. Bent said that our national symbol was "a fine looking bird, but one hardly worth the distinction." Not content with that put-down, he continued in the unrepentantly anthropomorphic style of the 1930s: "Its carrion-feeding habits, its timid and cowardly behavior, and its predatory attacks on the smaller and weaker osprey hardly inspire respect and certainly do not exemplify the best in American character."

Meanwhile, the hawk has vanished, leaving only the white-headed eagle soaring above us. Maybe I'm a sucker for image, but this majestic-looking bird seems a better national emblem than the lumbering wild turkey. And I'm not so sure about the "arrant coward" bit either. This eagle may not have been protecting its chick from the hawk, but it might have been—and it's pleasing to think that it was.

There is one fact about the bald eagle on which all naturalists agree: the mainstay of its diet is fish, freshly caught or hijacked from an osprey. Consequently, eagles are never far from water, and this one's presence reminds me that, although this trail is landlocked, we are surrounded by lakes. As Elton said, animals can tell us much about habitat.

As we walk, I expound on Elton's theories to Diane. When we stop to rest at the Buster Island campsites, a raccoon spies us, climbs down a small tree, and waits expectantly near a picnic table. "Just as Elton would have predicted," I say. "Picnic grounds are perfect coon habitat."

"Aren't you carrying this Elton stuff too far?"

"Elton's work is a cornerstone of modern ecology."

Diane rolls her eyes. "Let's get going."

Beyond the campsites, the trail enters a lovely live-oak hammock. We pass huge oaks, broad and squat and so verdurous with resurrection ferns that their limbs look like fuzzy green logs suspended in space. The shade is dense, and only a few rays of sunlight make it to the saw-palmetto understory.

Though the hammock is spectacular, it is small, and the trail soon breaks out into more open country. Tiger Lake is visible through a veil of trees. Then the trees drop away.

A gray and dull green jungle of head-high saw palmettos, wax myrtles, fetterbushes, and scrub oaks spreads to the horizon, broken only by a smattering of lonesome-looking pines. Tree swallows sail across the top of the brush, snapping up insects. I fall into my old habit of trying to name each plant we pass in order to identify the habitat. Is this scrub or dry prairie? I'm not sure.

The question is answered a moment later when a long-tailed gray-and-blue bird lands in a bush in front of us and begins eating berries.

"What is it?" Diane whispers.

"Scrub," I reply.

"I meant the bird, dummy."

"Scrub jay," I say. "An Eltonian 'exclusive' to this habitat."

Perhaps because their name sounds drab and their habitat is drab, the beauty of scrub jays always surprises me. They look like black-masked blue jays without the crest or the attitude. I think of scrub jays as cocky and friendly, unlike wary, defiant blue jays, a thought that shows anthropomorphism didn't die in the 1930s.

In the eastern United States, the scrub jay, *Aphelocoma coerulescens*, is found only in the dry, prickly scrub of peninsular Florida. Though the bird we are watching is gobbling berries, its main food is the acorns of scrub oaks. According to one estimate, each jay eats six to eight thousand of them a year.

Though *A. coerulescens* is exclusive in Florida to the scrub ecosystem, these birds are also found in the West. The two populations were once classified as different species. The Florida scrub jay was known as *A. cyanea*; the Western species was called the California jay, *A. californica californica*, though it is found as far east as Texas. Today, both jays are recognized as members of a single species and go by the same common and scientific names. Which leads to a question: how did two populations of the same species become separated by a thousand or more miles?

The answer is probably climate change. In the early Pleistocene Epoch, about two and a half million years ago, North America was considerably warmer and drier than it is now. The animals and plants that covered much of the continent resembled those found today on the African veldt. A broad swath of dry, scrublike lands extended from Florida to California. Elephants, ground sloths, and camels grazed this land—and scrub jays probably flitted through the brush. (There is no direct evidence that scrub jays existed in their present form two million years ago, but other members of the crow family have been around for longer than that.)

Alternating periods of cold and hot weather hit the continent later in the Pleistocene. As the climate of eastern North America became cooler and wetter, scrublands shrank in size, and only a few ecological "islands" of this ancient habitat survived in the East, all of them in Florida. Today, the scrub jays that inhabit these "islands" are cut off from one another—and from the larger population of jays that continues to exist in the arid regions of California and the Southwest.

The jay we are watching finishes its berries and flies off. Suddenly, the scrub seems a dreary place. We move along slowly. Lake Kissimmee is a great park for birders, and I'm hoping to see one other bird here. The Kissimmee prairie is known for its sandhill cranes.

I've only seen sandhill cranes (*Grus canadensis*) once before in

Florida. Two stately gray birds—specks, actually—were grazing a prairie in the Everglades. Although I was several hundred yards from them, they flew as soon as they saw me. Later, I discovered that this skittishness is normal for sandhill cranes. Even Audubon had trouble getting close to them, as he noted in his writings:

> The wariness of this species is so remarkable, that it takes all the cunning and care of an Indian hunter to approach it at times, especially in the case of an old bird. The acuteness of their sight and hearing is quite wonderful. If they perceive a man approaching, even at the distance of a quarter of a mile, they are sure to take wing.

No one is ever going to confuse my stealthiness with that of an Indian hunter, but I figure that the relative abundance of these birds on the Kissimmee prairie might give me a chance to get within binocular range of them. So we poke along through the scrub, eyes peeled for cranes.

Near the end of the walk, the scrub gives way to mowed fields. Cranes love corn and wheat, so I stop to scan the fields every few minutes. I spot crows, meadowlarks, and hundreds of tree swallows, but no cranes.

On the way out, we stop at the park entrance to say good-bye to George Aycrigg, the assistant park manager. I tell him about the wildlife we've seen—and the cranes we missed.

"Cranes?" he asks. "You want to see cranes? Come with me."

He leads us to the front of the entrance station. Two sandhill cranes are feeding in the grass. They are spectacular birds, nearly four feet tall, with red topknots, gray bodies, and long legs. I walk to within six feet of one. The bird that Audubon considered one of the wariest creatures in North America ignores me.

We watch them for a while, then Diane begins snapping pictures. I kneel on the ground to see what they're eating.

"How would Elton explain this?" she asks between shots.

"Chicken feed," I answer. "These birds are eating chicken feed."

Aycrigg grins knowingly but volunteers nothing.

I take a few photographs myself. When we get back to Orlando, I'm going to look up a silver-haired woman and show her how to identify the chicken-feed ecosystem. And I won't mention a single plant.

BEFORE YOU GO

For More Information
Lake Kissimmee State Park
14248 Camp Mack Road
Lake Wales, FL 33853
(941) 696-1112

Accommodations
Lake Wales is 19 miles west of the park. It has several motels.
Contact

Lake Wales Chamber of Commerce
P.O. Box 191
Lake Wales, FL 33859
(941) 676-7963

Campgrounds
A dirt road leads to the park's 60 campsites, which are tucked
away in the saw palmettos beneath the pines.

Maps
The free trail map handed out by the park is all that is needed
for these well-marked trails.

Fees
The park charges a $3.25 entrance fee per car. A fee schedule

for campsites and cabins is available.

Special Note

Park rules prohibit the feeding of wild animals, which can become dependent on "people food" and eventually lose their fear of humans and become nuisances. Nonetheless, some folks can't resist the temptation. The chicken feed we discovered in the grass at the ranger station was apparently scattered there by such a person. Neither I nor the park rangers encourage this activity.

More about Scrub

In this part of Florida, the pure scrub ecosystem is found on the Lake Wales Ridge, a few miles west of the park. The ecosystem at Lake Kissimmee that I call "scrub" is, technically speaking, scrubby flatwoods, a transition zone between the pine flatwoods and pure scrub. Scrubby flatwoods occur at slightly lower elevations and on less well-drained soil than scrub. The flora and fauna of these ecosystems are so similar that it is hard to distinguish between the two. Even the scrub jay—which is picky about where it lives—is equally at home in both habitats.

Points of Interest

Just north of the Buster Island loop is the 5.6-mile North Loop Trail. I haven't walked this trail, but it looks inviting.

The Lake Kissimmee region is cow country, and on weekends and holidays, the park's cow camp re-creates the lives of the people and cattle that roamed these prairies in 1876. A "cow hunter" moves cows from one place to another with a 15-foot leather whip, with which he produces sharp cracks that sound like gunshots.

Additional Reading

Animal Ecology by Charles Elton, October House, New York, 1966. This volume is a reissue of the original book, which was published in Great Britain in 1927.

Audubon in Florida by Kathryn Hall Proby, University of Miami Press, Coral Gables, 1974.

Birds of America by T. Gilbert Pearson, Garden City Books, Garden City, New York, 1936.

The Florida Scrub Jay by Glen E. Woolfenden and John W. Fitzpatrick, Princeton University Press, Princeton, New Jersey, 1984.

"Florida's Scrub Jay" by Jeff Ripple, *Florida Wildlife* 48, May–June 1994, 14–15.

Life Histories of North American Birds of Prey, part 1, by Arthur Cleveland Bent, Dover Publications, New York, 1961. This book was originally published in 1937 as the Smithsonian Institution's *Bulletin 167*.

Life and Death in the Salt Marsh

Cruickshank Trail
Merritt Island National Wildlife Refuge

Merritt Island National Wildlife Refuge lies east of Titusville and just north of the Kennedy Space Center. Its 139,305 acres are bordered on the west by the Indian River and on the east by Mosquito Lagoon and Canaveral National Seashore.

From Titusville, take S.R. 402 east over the Indian River into the refuge. About 3 miles from town, turn left on S.R. 406. Follow it to Black Point Drive, a self-guided automobile tour route. The trail begins at stop number 8.

Cruickshank Trail loops around Black Point Marsh. To walk it clockwise (as we did), go left at the trailhead.

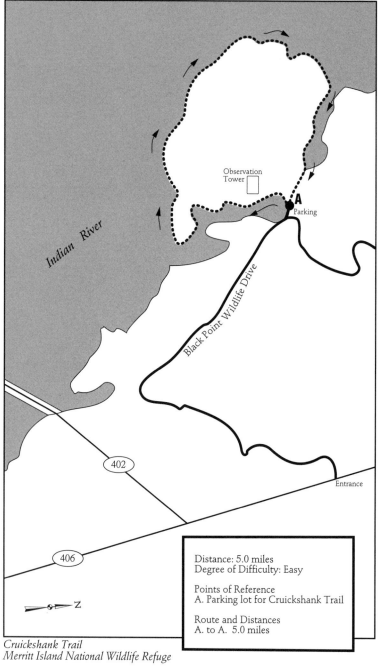

Indian River

Observation
Tower

A
Parking

Black Point Wildlife Drive

402

406

Entrance

N

Distance: 5.0 miles
Degree of Difficulty: Easy

Points of Reference
A. Parking lot for Cruickshank Trail

Route and Distances
A. to A. 5.0 miles

Cruickshank Trail
Merritt Island National Wildlife Refuge

Sharing a planet with human beings can be risky. We have knocked off our fellow species with abandon. We easily disposed of the dire wolf, the Jamaican iguana, and the ivory-billed woodpecker and, without much more effort, reduced billions of passenger pigeons to one, which died in a cage at the Cincinnati Zoo in 1914. However, humans aren't perfect predators, and some animal seriously challenges us every now and then. When that happens, a fierce struggle ensues.

You can see the results of one such struggle along Cruickshank Trail at Merritt Island National Wildlife Refuge. As you walk the trail, what you see—and don't see—has been affected by a take-no-prisoners war. Here, fifty years ago, *Homo sapiens* squared off against *Aedes solicitans*. The battle between man and salt-marsh mosquito is winding down now, and a tenuous truce is in place. Men and mosquitoes both survived, but there were winners and losers nonetheless.

It's nine o'clock on a January morning. Back home, folks are digging out from a two-day blizzard that dumped a foot or more of snow on much of the Atlantic seaboard. The television this morning showed the usual skidding cars, houses with snow drifts up to the eaves, and thermometers displaying below-zero temperatures. The weather's better here at the start of Cruickshank Trail. It's sunny and about sixty-five degrees. Instead of a snow-covered landscape, a mosaic of canals, creeks, impoundments, and brown marsh grass spreads out in front of us. Scattered cabbage-palm hammocks rise from the marsh, and pine flatlands loom in the distance.

"This beats the software business, doesn't it?" I ask Diane, remembering gray winter mornings in a colder climate. She mutters something about enjoying the sunshine but missing the paydays, then starts down the trail.

The sandy path follows a dike between a grassy marsh and an impoundment rimmed with black mangroves and tall, green leather ferns. It looks like water-bird heaven, and it is. White ibises, tri-colored herons, great blue herons, and a reddish egret stalk fish in the impoundment; a kingfisher perches in a mangrove above the dark waters of a canal; and acrobatic tree swallows sail above the marsh, picking off insects.

As we walk, unseen creatures slide off the dike and splash into the water in front of us. Dark dragonflies dart across the impoundment, and a marsh rabbit bounds across the path and disappears into the grass. A line of brown pelicans flaps east toward the sea.

All of these plants and animals were present in the 1940s, when the state of Florida fired the first shot in the Great Mosquito War. At that time, there were no dikes and no impoundments on Merritt Island. The salt marsh was interrupted only by occasional creeks. Most of the island was high marsh, which stayed dry for long periods and flooded only when the wind combined with unusually high tides to blow in water from the Indian River. (Low marsh is flooded by high tides twice a day.) High marsh, it turns out, is ideal breeding habitat for salt-marsh mosquitoes.

A. solicitans lays its eggs on mud flats or moist ground. When rising water hydrates them, the eggs hatch. Even in a state famous for its mosquitoes, Merritt Island's marshes were considered scary places. In one of the yuckiest tests imaginable, the Brevard County Mosquito Control Unit reported landings of five hundred mosquitoes per minute on one person, the highest number ever recorded anywhere. Residents slapped mosquitoes and stuffed newspapers under their clothes. Clearly, the mosquitoes of Merritt Island were more than holding their own, but Florida had recently added a new weapon to its mosquito-fighting arsenal, one far more potent than a slap.

In 1939, a Swiss chemist named Paul Muller had synthesized and tested a new insecticide called DDT, for which he won a Nobel Prize in 1948. But long before the Nobel was awarded, Florida and other states were spraying DDT on marshes and agricultural fields.

The initial results were spectacular: food production skyrocketed, insect-borne diseases declined, and Merritt Island became habitable.

As we continue along the trail, we spot more and more birds. Two not-very-roseate roseate spoonbills wade the shallows, pink-tinged bundles of pale feathers set atop skinny legs; a flock of pintails floats in the center of the impoundment; and two royal terns dive repeatedly into the gray water and emerge with tiny silvery fish in their orange beaks. American coots are everywhere, and Gulf fritillaries flutter up and down the trail on bright orange wings, stopping now and then to suck nectar from the white flowers of Spanish needles.

Clumped cordgrass (*Spartina bakerii*), black needlerush (*Juncus roemerianus*), and saltwort (*Distichlis spiculata*) dominate the salt marsh, and red-winged blackbirds flit from stalk to stalk. A light breeze from the east carries the tangy scent of open ocean. The whine of an occasional mosquito reminds me that a truce implies coexistence. And coexisting with these insects is no fun.

An attack by hungry salt-marsh mosquitoes can drive a grown man crazy. But as bad as they are, they are not the real villains of the mosquito world. That distinction belongs to anopheline mosquitoes, which act as vectors for malaria, and to *Aedes aegypti*, which transmits yellow fever and dengue. Even among experts, though, the salt-marsh mosquito has a bad reputation. Robert Matheson, the author of *Handbook of the Mosquitoes of North America*, says, "They are fierce biters and attack in the open sunlight as well as during the evening hours and at night." In other words, they'll suck your blood at any time, day or night.

The success of DDT was short-lived. By the mid-1950s, DDT-resistant strains of mosquitoes were evolving, and Floridians were beginning to suspect that the insecticide had something to do with plummeting populations of bald eagles, brown pelicans, ospreys, and other wildlife. But men and mosquitoes—at least in the numbers found on Merritt Island—could not live together. Something had to be done.

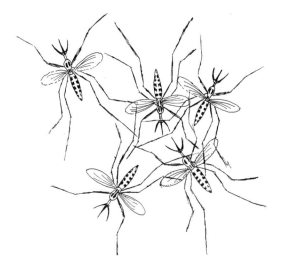

It's not clear who came up with the idea of building dikes and flooding the marshes, but it was someone who knew mosquitoes. Since salt-marsh mosquitoes lay their eggs only on damp ground, flooding stops them from reproducing. In 1954, engineers began diking Merritt Island and flooding the high marshes. The technique proved to be almost as effective as DDT. From 1950 to 1960, the number of mosquitoes in Brevard County dropped precipitously, while the human population rose 370 percent. By the time NASA began buying land in 1962 for a space center on Merritt Island, the mosquitoes that had plagued the region for centuries appeared to be under control.

By now, we have walked halfway around the impoundment, and the temperature has climbed well above seventy. The marsh here is drier, with little open water. Sanderlings probe the mud, and immature white ibises search the flats for fiddler crabs. The distinctive sweet-and-sour odor of salt marsh rises from the brown cordgrass that borders the mud flats. Though we stop frequently to admire the wading birds present in almost every patch of open water, the walk goes quickly.

Near the end of the loop, Cruickshank Trail passes a long board-walk that leads to a weathered blind near the center of the impoundment. We walk toward it on gray boards spattered with white droppings. Suddenly, a flock of pintails pops out of the water to our right. We take a few more steps and another flock—this one of blue-winged teals—takes to the air to our left. Then raft after raft of ducks rise from the impoundment, filling the sky with noise and motion.

By the time we reach the blind, there is not a duck in sight. Only one bird is left, a tricolored heron in full breeding plumage. We sit in the blind for a long time watching the heron prance around in the shallow water. He doesn't appear to be searching for food, but merely showing off and enjoying himself. Finally, he, too, flies off, and we are alone in the blind. The emptiness reminds me of the one bird we haven't seen today, a bird no one will ever see again.

Banning DDT on Merritt Island and flooding the marshes bene-fited most bird species. Free from regular DDT sprayings, raptors and pelicans began a long, slow comeback, and wading birds and waterfowl flocked to the open waters of the impoundments. But the flooding had a profound effect on the ecosystem, and some of the plants and wildlife of the salt marsh didn't fare as well.

In a 1964 paper published in the journal *Mosquito News*, B. W. Clements and A. J. Rogers of the Entomological Research Center of the Florida State Board of Health presented the results of their work on the impoundment of salt-water marshes. Their photographs documented the death of the marsh. In permanently impounded areas, cattails and other invading species replaced the cordgrass, needlerush, and saltwort of the marshes. Just as DDT spraying of the marshes had unintended side effects, so did flooding.

Still, it was unlikely that the impounding would be reversed because cattails were displacing salt grass. Mosquito control was more important than a few plants, none of them rare or endangered. It took a small, secretive bird to bring the problems caused by the flooding to the attention of the public.

The frontispiece of Arthur Cleveland Bent's *Life Histories of North American Cardinals, Grosbeaks, Buntings, Towhees, Finches, Sparrows, and Allies* is a painting of three dusky seaside sparrows. It shows a black-and-white-striped bird with tiny yellow patches above its eyes and on its wings. For years, this sparrow was considered a separate species, *Ammospiza nigrescens*; today, it is classified as a subspecies, *Ammodramus maritimus nigrescens*. Duskies were never numerous, and they had a very restricted range: they were found only in salt marshes within a ten-mile radius of Titusville. The biggest colony was on Merritt Island.

The duskies fed primarily on insects and spiders, and as with all meat eaters, the DDT sprayed on the marshes accumulated in their systems. By the mid-1950s, the number of breeding pairs dropped from two thousand to six hundred. Not many people noticed. Pelicans, eagles, and ospreys were disappearing, too, and nobody had time to worry about a tiny marsh bird that almost no one ever saw. When diking and flooding replaced DDT as the primary mosquito-control method, osprey and eagle populations rebounded, but the duskies continued to decline.

The problem, of course, was that the marsh was no longer a

marsh but an impoundment. Duskies—along with the equally secretive but more widespread rails and bitterns—were the only birds that nested *exclusively* in salt marsh. One of Bent's correspondents said that he "considered the [duskies'] ideal nesting habitat to be a damp, but not flooded, salt marsh dotted with small open ponds." When the marshes around Titusville were flooded, the one place in the world where duskies nested disappeared.

After Merritt Island National Wildlife Refuge was created in 1963 on land owned by NASA, the biologists working here recognized the plight of the duskies. In 1969, the refuge removed some of the dikes on Merritt Island in an attempt to re-create nesting habitat for the sparrows. Twelve years later, biologists began a new program aimed at restoring much of the original salt marsh. They used a technique called rotary ditching to breech many of the dikes. This let the water level in the impoundments rise and fall with the natural fluctuations of the river, allowing the marsh to function more naturally. Rotary ditching was also used to dig canals to connect those areas of the refuge that were below mean low water. This let fish move into and out of the impoundments as water levels rose and fell. The fish eat mosquito larvae and substantially reduce their numbers.

Rotary ditching appears to be working. Cattails are not as abundant at the refuge as they were ten years ago. Mosquitoes are more common but tolerable; a dab or two of repellent will protect most hikers. And the diverse habitats—the enclosed and breached impoundments, canals, and tidal creeks and the restored salt marshes that are the result of our war on mosquitoes—attract a startling array of birds, though bitterns and rails are still scarce.

Unfortunately, the changes came too late for the duskies. By 1969, only thirty-five pairs were left on the refuge, and the last dusky seaside sparrow seen in the wild was spotted near

ational Seashore lies north and east of the wildlife
erpiece is Klondike Beach, a 12-mile-long stretch
oped Atlantic shoreline that can be reached only
en the wildlife refuge and Klondike Beach is the
osquito Lagoon, one of the great trout-fishing spots
enjoy it, take your best spinning rod—and your

ading

k's Photographs of Birds of America by Allan D.
Dover Publications, New York, 1977.

f the Mosquitoes of North America by Robert Matheson,
blishing Company, Ithaca, New York, 1944.

ng Salt Marshes for Mosquito Control . . . and Its
d Life" by Maurice W. Provost, *Florida Naturalist 32*,
, 163–70.

ies of North American Cardinals, Grosbeaks, Buntings,
es, Sparrows, and Allies, part 2, by Arthur Cleveland
aborators, Dover Publications, New York, 1968.

l History of Mosquitoes by Marston Bates, Macmillan
ew York, 1949.

eductions in Salt-Marsh Control: Past and Future"
. Provost, *Mosquito News* 37, December 1977, 689–98.

f Impounding for the Control of Salt-Marsh Mos-
orida, 1958–1963" by B. W. Clements, Jr., and An-
rs, *Mosquito News* 24, September 1964, 265–76.

Cruickshank Trail in 1977. By then, a few birds had been placed in a captive breeding program, but it was to no avail. In a finale eerily reminiscent of that of the passenger pigeon, the last dusky seaside sparrow died in a cage at Disney World in 1987.

BEFORE YOU GO

For More Information
Merritt Island National Wildlife Refuge
P.O. Box 6504
Titusville, FL 32782
(407) 861-0667

Accommodations
Merritt Island National Wildlife Refuge is just across the Indian River from Titusville, which offers a range of accommodations. Contact

Titusville Area Chamber of Commerce
2000 South Washington Avenue
Titusville, FL 32780
(407) 267-3036

Campgrounds
Camping is not permitted at the refuge, but there are several commercial campgrounds in the Titusville area. For a list, contact the chamber of commerce.

Back-country camping is allowed in Canaveral National Seashore,

which adjoins the refuge. For more information, contact
Canaveral National Seashore
308 Julia Street
Titusville, FL 32780
(407) 267-1110

Maps

A map of Cruickshank Trail is in the refuge's free brochure, *Black Point Drive*.

Fees

The refuge asks for a $1 donation at the beginning of Black Point Drive. It's the best bargain in the state.

Special Precautions

Parts of the refuge and the national seashore are closed on or around launch days at Kennedy Space Center. You may want to check with the refuge about launch dates before you visit.

More about Allan D. Cruickshank (1907–74)

The man for whom Cruickshank Trail is named played a key role in establishing Merritt Island National Wildlife Refuge. Allan Cruickshank was an ornithologist, a naturalist, and a staff photographer for the National Audubon Society for 36 years. He and his wife, Helen, were living in nearby Rockledge in 1962 when NASA acquired the northern half of Merritt Island for its space center. Much of NASA's land was intended to buffer the space center's operational areas from civilian encroachment. Cruickshank wanted to use the buffer zone as a wildlife-protection area.

The task was a daunting one. The United States was locked into the Cold War with the Soviet Union, and the "race for space" was deemed an important front in that war. Preserving wildlife

---

was not one of NASA's pr
Somehow, though, Cru
2,500 acres of marshland ov
life Service. Those marshes
National Wildlife Refuge. O
the wildlife service transfer
Park Service, which establis

Who *was* Allan Cruicksha
so we have to rely on the
Cruickshank's Photographs of
of his superb black-and-whi
shot of Cruickshank in the
attention. It was taken by h
man with close-cropped bl
climbing a steep, rocky cliff i
supporting himself with a r
graphing a raven's nest.

In the photo, Allan Cruic
purposeful. It is the face of
doing. He must have had th
when he convinced the bu
agencies that a wildlife refug
To a large extent, Merritt Isl
legacy, one for which we sho

Points of Interest

The wildlife refuge is surro
To the south is the Kennedy
center that is open to the pu
right day (as by chance we or
ing placidly in the Indian Rive
its launch pad and soars into t

Canaveral
refuge. Its cer
of never-deve
by foot. Betw
aptly named
in the state.
best repellent

Additional R

Cruicksha
Cruickshank,

Handbook
Comstock P

"Impound
Effects on B
October 195

Life Histor
Towhees, Fin
Bent and co

The Natur
Company, N

"Source
by Maurice

"Studies
quitoes in
drew J. Rog

Big Scrub

Florida National Scenic Trail
Ocala National Forest

Ocala National Forest lies northwest of Orlando between Ocala and Daytona Beach. Within its boundaries are 430,446 acres, 382,664 of which are owned by the United States Forest Service; the other lands are inholdings. S.R. 40, which runs east and west, bisects the national forest.

The trailhead for this walk is on S.R. 40 about 25 miles east of Ocala, just south of Juniper Springs Recreation Area. All 6.7 miles of this walk are on the Florida National Scenic Trail, which will be 1,300 miles long when completed. A 67-mile segment of this footpath runs from the northern edge to the southern boundary of Ocala National Forest.

From S.R. 40, a well-marked trail leads south into Big Scrub, the best example of sand-pine scrub in the state. This walk continues past Farles Prairie and Farles Lake and ends on S.R. 595. Unless you have someone to meet you, as I did, you will have to retrace your footsteps to the trailhead.

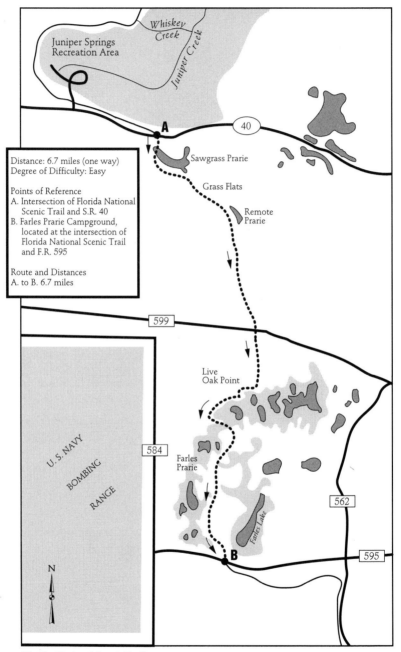

Whiskey Creek

Juniper Creek

Juniper Springs
Recreation Area

A

40

Sawgrass Prarie

Grass Flats

Remote
Prarie

Distance: 6.7 miles (one way)
Degree of Difficulty: Easy

Points of Reference
A. Intersection of Florida National
   Scenic Trail and S.R. 40
B. Farles Prarie Campground,
   located at the intersection of
   Florida National Scenic Trail
   and F.R. 595

Route and Distances
A. to B. 6.7 miles

599

Live
Oak Point

U. S. NAVY

BOMBING

RANGE

584

Farles
Prarie

562

Farles Lake

B

595

N

Florida National Scenic Trail
Ocala National Forest

An eerie, high-pitched moan comes from the scrawny pines. Enigmatic orange mounds and puffy gray lumps sit atop the dead pine needles that cover the sandy path. A bird calls from the brush, a harsh sound that is similar to but not identical to the cry of a blue jay. Oddball oaks crowd the path; they are short and scrubby, with leathery down-curved leaves that are similar to but not identical to those of a live oak. I turn around and head back to the car; I've seen enough. My scouting trip to Ocala National Forest's Big Scrub country is complete. Do I want to hike this trail tomorrow? You bet I do.

Some people find the scrub country dry and thorny and altogether unattractive. Others love it. Marjorie Kinnan Rawlings set her Pulitzer Prize–winning novel, *The Yearling*, in Big Scrub. Penny Baxter, the father of Jody, the boy who adopts the fawn around which the story is built, moved to the scrub because "something in him was raw and tender. The touch of men was hurtful upon it, but the touch of the pines was healing."

Rawlings herself lived in Cross Creek, about twenty-five miles northwest of Big Scrub. Cross Creek was her refuge, as Big Scrub was Penny's. But my affair with scrub arose from something quite different. To me, scrub is inscrutable and mysterious, like my first glimpse of the calculus or *Ulysses*. And it engenders in me a hankering to know more. I only scratched the surface of this ecosystem during my walk in the Lake Wales scrub at Lake Kissimmee State Park; tomorrow, I plan to further my education.

It is a beautiful, clear January morning. The temperature is in the mid-sixties, and a gentle wind rattles the cabbage-palm fronds. From its trailhead on S.R. 40, Florida National Scenic Trail enters a palm hammock, passes a marshy lake, then ascends into the scrub.

Sunlight filters through the pines, dappling the understory of dull green scrub oaks and bright green saw palmettos. Robins fly through the underbrush, feeding on gallberries, and pine warblers flit through the dark green crowns of the pines. Though it rains three or four feet a year here, the sandy soil retains so little moisture that some writers have compared Big Scrub to a desert. Maybe they're right, but it's the greenest desert I've ever seen— and the only one with pine trees.

Egg-shaped gray lumps three or four inches tall grow beside the trail. The lumps are soft to the touch, and a dense mat of them resembles a foam rubber trail mattress. They look like moss, and their common name is reindeer moss. But these lumps are not mosses at all; they are lichens.

A dozen or more species of lichens grow in the scrub. Field guides almost always refer to these gray, airy lumps as *Cladonia* spp., meaning that they are undetermined species of the genus *Cladonia*. The lack of specificity is understandable; lichens are strange organisms. And the people who study them speak a strange language. Here is Ursula K. Duncan, describing the characteristics of lichens in the family Cladoniaceae: "The primary (basal) thallus is either squamulose or crustaceous, the secondary (upright) thallus consisting of a usually hollow podetium, that is, an enlarged stalk bearing the fruit or else sterile. Algal cells bright green. Spores colorless, ellipsoid to clavate, simple or septate."

The quote is taken from the book *A Guide to the Study of Lichens*, whose first sentence reads, "This book is intended for botanical students with no previous knowledge of the subject." In her defense, Duncan does define her terms elsewhere in the book. Nevertheless, I found the descriptions hard to follow.

In fact, the only book about lichens that I have been able to

understand at all is Mason E. Hale's *How to Know the Lichens*. From Hale, I learned that lichens are composed of two distinct organisms, an alga and a fungus, which live together symbiotically. Lichen symbiosis, though, differs from all other kinds in that a new plant body (called a thallus) is formed from the association. The thallus bears no resemblance to either the alga or the fungus; it is a composite organism that behaves as an independent plant—a lichen. In the laboratory, botanists are able to separate the alga and the fungus that make up some lichens, but they can rarely induce them to re-form into a lichen.

The *Cladonia* lichens along this trail are squamulose lichens that consist of small, separate lobelike structures. The lobelike structures look so soft that I decide to perform my own test. I lie down on a gray mat of lichens. "Squamulose lichens," I say into my tape recorder, as I wriggle around trying to get comfortable, "are not as firm as foam rubber and could serve as a mattress only in a pinch."

The trail enters an area of head-high brush, dense and impenetrable. Skinny pines rise above the brush and sway in the breeze. This is pure scrub, and the raspy cry of a scrub jay—which sounds like the call of an off-key blue jay—confirms my diagnosis. I slow down to examine the understory.

Some of the plants are easy to identify: gallberry, with its shiny black berries; saw palmetto, with its sawtooth leafstalks; Florida rosemary, whose dark green needles resemble those of a spruce; and the unmistakable prickly pear. But much of the vegetation along the trail is scrub oak, a name that covers a multitude of species.

I spot the broad, shining leaves of myrtle oak (*Quercus myrtifolia*) and the stiff, leathery, down-cupped leaves of a sand live oak (*Q. geminata*), which closely resemble those of an ordinary live oak. I know that Chapman's oak (*Q. chapmanii*) grows here, and probably runner oak (*Q. minima*) and other species. But the brush is so thick and the oaks so similar that one plant blurs into another, and I am unable to identify them even with the help of a field guide. When I said scrub is inscrutable, this vegetational blurring is what I had in mind.

As I walk, more of the strange moans I heard on my scouting trip come from the woods. It is a sound unlike any other I have ever heard. Finally, I spot the source: two pines beside the trail are swaying in the breeze and rubbing against one another. The trunks of these pines are so slender, so supple, and so close together that even the slightest whiff can cause one to bend and scrape its neighbor, something that sturdier pines rarely do. Indeed, these pines are different from the slash, loblolly, and longleaf pines found in most of the state. These are sand pines (*Pinus clausa*), and they distinguish the Ocala scrub from the Lake Wales scrub, where the only trees are widely scattered slash pines.

Sand pines grow only in Florida and a sliver of southern Alabama, usually in scrub. Their wispy trunks support small crowns thick with old cones. They clump together along the trail in even-aged stands. The sand pine is a short-lived species, with an average life span of about sixty-five years. They are fast-growing, however, and as an occasional clear-cut along this trail attests, they are logged to make pulp for paper.

Like longleaf-pine savanna, sand-pine scrub requires fire to maintain itself. But the type of fire the two ecosystems depend on is quite different. The pines of a longleaf savanna are widely spaced. Consequently, the periodic fires that race through them are usually ground fires that burn out the hardwoods but leave the fire-resistant pines. So dense are the trees and so dry is the understory in Big Scrub, however, that fires quickly escalate into catastrophes that blaze through the crowns of the pines and kill them. In 1935, a fire in the Ocala scrub burned thirty-five thousand acres in four hours.

But the sand pines and other plants of the scrub have adapted to catastrophe. Fire causes the old cones that cling to almost every tree to finally open and release their seeds on the ash-enriched soil, and the understory plants regenerate from their deep and extensive roots. The result is even-aged stands of sand pines growing above a healthy, rejuvenated scrub—exactly the landscape along much of this trail.

These periodic infernos should decimate the wildlife of the scrub, but like the sand pines, these animals have adapted to fire. I notice one sign of that adaptation as I walk. Piles of orange sand sit on the white sand of the trail. Near the halfway point of the walk, I stop to have lunch beside one of the piles. Between bites of a sandwich, I poke at the orange mound.

The sand is moist to the touch and grainy, and the hole from which it came is about the circumference of my little finger. Two questions immediately come to mind: why is the sand orange? and what creature dug it up?

The first question is easy. Regular summer downpours have leached the iron out of the top few inches of soil, leaving white sand on the surface. Beneath that, though, iron oxides color the sand a rusty orange. Some creature has dug a hole deep in the ground and carried the iron-rich subsoil to the surface.

The second question is not as easy. A dozen or more species protect themselves from fire by living beneath the white sand of Big Scrub. Gopher tortoises, scarab beetles, fire ants, and mice all dig burrows here, as do armadillos and other creatures. This particular hole appears to be the right size for a large beetle, but short of digging it out, there's no way to know for sure. Mysterious, fireproof lives are being lived beneath my feet, but I have little idea of what those lives are like.

I try a process of elimination. This hole is too small to be a gopher-tortoise or armadillo hole, so I can eliminate those possibilities. I run my fingers through the orange sand. Because I don't feel any sharp, terrible bites, I can also eliminate fire ants. But my line of reasoning won't take me any farther, so I get up and start walking again.

Near the end of the walk, the trail passes several large lakes. Turtles with shining black carapaces sun themselves on islands, and a yellow-bellied sapsucker taps on a tree near the trail. A tall man in tattered brown shorts and an even more tattered gray T-shirt comes up the path toward me. His boots are worn, and gray stubble covers his deeply tanned face. He is the first person I've seen in the scrub today, so I stop to chat.

We introduce ourselves. His name is Daniel, and he is from Maine. Daniel is a campground host at Farles Prairie Campground, and he has spent the last three winters here on the edge of Big Scrub. He is going to check out a large alligator someone reported seeing in a nearby lake.

I ask Daniel about the names of the scrub oaks.

"This is a wonderful place to spend the winter," he says softly, "but the only plants I recognize for sure are saw palmettos, which I stay away from, and blueberries, which I know 'cause I pick 'em in the spring."

"The oaks are especially hard to identify," I say. "Probably take a botanist to sort them out."

"Everything in the scrub is hard to figure out," he says, edging by me on the trail. "But I love it. It's quiet and peaceful. A good place to retire to."

"It's also mysterious and inscrutable," I say, more to myself than to his retreating back.

He hears me and stops to wave good-bye. "Ayuh," he says. "That, too."

BEFORE YOU GO

For More Information

Seminole Ranger District
Ocala National Forest
40929 State Road 19
Umatilla, FL 32784
(352) 669-3153

or

Lake George Ranger District
Ocala National Forest
17147 East State Road 40
Silver Springs, FL 34488
(352) 625-2520

Ocala National Forest also has two visitor information centers.
Contact

Forest Visitor Center and Bookstore
10863 East FL 40
Silver Springs, FL 34488
(352) 625-7470

Forest Pittman Visitor Center
45621 State Road 19
Altoona, FL 32702
(352) 669-7495

Accommodations

Ocala National Forest covers a sizable patch of north-central
Florida. The trailhead for this walk is about 25 miles west of Ocala,
which has numerous hotels and motels. Contact

Ocala-Marion Chamber of Commerce
110 East Silver Springs Boulevard
Ocala, FL 33470
(352) 629-8051

Campgrounds

Twenty-two campgrounds are scattered across the national forest.

Juniper Springs Recreation Area has 79 campsites and is less than a mile from the trailhead for this walk. (See the "Points of Interest" section for more about this recreation area.)

The walk ends at Farles Prairie Campground, a primitive camping area limited to no more than 75 campers at one time. If Juniper Springs is the Waldorf-Astoria, then Farles Prairie is a Motel 6. Nonetheless, the campers here during my visit appeared to be enjoying themselves—and spending less money. Campsites at Juniper Springs are around $13 a night; those at Farles Prairie are free.

Neither campground takes reservations.

Maps

The best trail map for this walk is "Florida National Scenic Trail," issued by the Ocala National Forest Interpretive Association. The map shows the Ocala section of Florida National Scenic Trail and is available from the visitor centers for $3.

To navigate the logging roads that crisscross the national forest, I recommend buying a copy of the map "Ocala National Forest." It can be obtained for $4 from the visitor centers.

Fees

There is no entrance fee for the national forest, but some of the recreation areas charge a day-use fee.

Points of Interest

Juniper Springs Recreation Area lies just north of the intersection of Florida National Scenic Trail and S.R. 40. Two springs, Juniper and Fern Hammock, are the main attractions. From them flow 13 million gallons of clear, 72-degree water every day. Swimming and snorkeling are permitted in Juniper Springs, and a short nature trail will introduce you to the plants and trees of the area.

The best way to see the Juniper Springs region is by canoe. Juniper Creek, a 7-mile spring run, leads from the springs to Lake George. The creek passes through Juniper Prairie Wilderness, a swampy wetland with cypresses and wading birds and alligators. Canoes can be rented at the recreation area.

Additional Reading

"Along a Ridge in Florida, an Ecological House Built on Sand" by Don Stap, *Smithsonian* 25, September 1994, 36–44.

Cross Creek and *The Yearling* by Marjorie Kinnan Rawlings. Both were published by Charles Scribner's Sons, *Cross Creek* in 1942 and *The Yearling* in 1940.

"Florida Scrub" by D. Bruce Means, *Florida Wildlife* 48, May–June 1994, 10–13.

A Guide to the Study of Lichens by Ursula K. Duncan, Arbroath T. Buncle and Company, Printers and Publishers, Market Place, Great Britain, 1959.

How to Know the Lichens, 2nd edition, by Mason E. Hale, William C. Brown Company Publishers, Dubuque, Iowa.

"Last Stand in the Sand" by Mark Deyrup and Thomas Eisner, *Natural History* 102, December 1993, 42–47.

Marjorie Kinnan Rawlings by Samuel I. Bellman, Twayne Publishers, New York, 1974.

Scrub Plant Guide: A Pocket Guide to the Common Plants of Southern Florida's Scrub Community by Daniel Austin, Gumbo Limbo Nature Center of South Palm Beach County, 1993. This is the only guide to scrub vegetation I have run into. It is a valuable addition to the libraries of naturalists who want to educate themselves about the scrub ecosystem.

NORTHEAST

I made a tour round the south point of the island, walking the shelly
paved sea beach, and picking up novelties.
WILLIAM BARTRAM, 1791

A Walk with Billy

Gainesville-Hawthorne and La Chua Trails
Paynes Prairie State Preserve

Paynes Prairie is a 21,000-acre state preserve south of Gainesville. This walk begins at the trailhead for Gainesville-Hawthorne State Trail in Boulware Springs Park, located at 3300 Southeast 15th Street in Gainesville.

Gainesville-Hawthorne State Trail runs east along the northern rim of the prairie. Just beyond the 1-mile marker is a pathway that goes to La Chua Trail, which leads south past Alachua Sink and Alachua Lake into the heart of the preserve. At the end of the trail is an observation platform that offers good views of the prairie and its wildlife. Return by the same route.

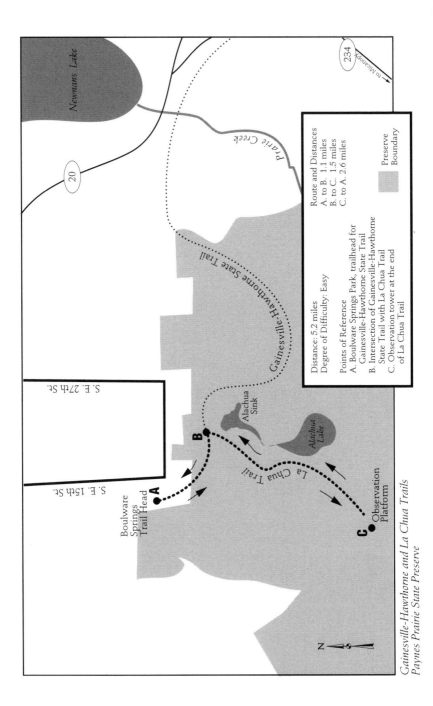

Gainesville-Hawthorne and La Chua Trails
Paynes Prairie State Preserve

Distance: 5.2 miles
Degree of Difficulty: Easy

Points of Reference
A. Boulware Springs Park, trailhead for
   Gainesville-Hawthorne State Trail
B. Intersection of Gainesville-Hawthorne
   State Trail with La Chua Trail
C. Observation tower at the end
   of La Chua Trail

Route and Distances
A. to B. 1.1 miles
B. to C. 1.5 miles
C. to A. 2.6 miles

Preserve
Boundary

Newnans Lake

Prairie Creek

234
to Micanopy

20

S.E. 27th St.

S.E. 15th St.

Boulware
Springs
Trail Head

A

B

Alachua
Sink

Alachua
Lake

La Chua Trail

Gainesville-Hawthorne State Trail

C

Observation
Platform

N

In 1772, William Bartram, near bankruptcy after a series of failed business ventures, renounced commerce and decided on a career in botany. He found a sponsor, Dr. John Fothergill, a wealthy London physician with interests in art and science. Fothergill offered to pay him to collect specimens and make drawings of the plants and wildlife of Florida. Bartram jumped at the chance. He left his home near Philadelphia in April 1773 for Charleston, South Carolina. By May, he was in Florida.

Although Europeans had occupied the coastal fringes of Florida for 250 years before Bartram's journey, the interior remained largely unexplored. Bartram spent much of 1773 and 1774 roaming this territory, often alone or with Indians, making notes on and drawings of what he saw. All his life, he had been known as Billy Bartram, but the Seminoles called him Puc Puggy—"the Flower Hunter."

After almost two years in Florida and Georgia, Bartram obtained Dr. Fothergill's approval for another trip, and in 1775, he headed for Cherokee country. He toured North and South Carolina, then proceeded to Mobile. He left the South for good in December 1777 and arrived in Pennsylvania a month later.

Within a few years, he finished the manuscript of *Travels through North & South Carolina, Georgia, East & West Florida, the Cherokee Country, the Extensive Territories of the Muscogulges, or Creek Confederacy, and the Country of the Chactaws.* The book was published in Philadelphia in 1791. It was not an immediate bestseller in this country but did much better abroad. Within ten years of its publication, nine editions of *Travels* appeared in Europe. The book influenced Wordsworth and Coleridge. Parts of "Kubla Khan" were based on *Travels.* The well-known lines, "Where Alph, the sacred river ran/Through caverns measureless to man/Down to a sunless sea," were based on Bartram's descriptions of Florida karst, the puzzle of underground rivers and springs that riddles the limestone beneath the state. Wordsworth's poem "Ruth" also borrowed heavily from *Travels.*

Over the years, more and more readers on this side of the Atlantic came to appreciate Bartram's lyrical prose and careful observations. Today, *Travels* is regarded as a classic of North American natural history, as important as the journals of Lewis and Clark and John Wesley Powell's *Report on the Exploration of the Colorado River.*

Because early accounts of Florida's natural history are rare and sketchy, Bartram's *Travels* is particularly important to Floridians. It defines what the state was like before condominiums, golf courses, malls, and freeways. As one historian put it, "His observations have served for 200 years as the primary text on the natural life of Florida." These days, Florida's state parks, even the highly developed ones, call themselves "the *Real* Florida," but if a natural area looks the way Bartram described it, Floridians give it a higher honor: they call it "Old Florida." (For more on this, see the next chapter.)

I have long been a fan of Bartram. I acquired a copy of *Travels* decades ago. I didn't read it straight through, but dipped into it when the mood struck or when I needed information. By now, I have read it all, parts of it many times. His readers grow to enjoy the company of the man in a way they could never enjoy a real travel companion. Bartram doesn't snore at night like a real person might. He doesn't walk fast when you want to walk slow or talk when you want to be quiet. He doesn't demand tea when you want coffee. He is knowledgeable, but not in a know-it-all way, and he is always good-natured and adventurous. He is, in fact, the perfect travel companion.

For that reason, I love to tuck a copy of *Travels* in my pack and visit the places Bartram wrote about over two centuries ago. I like to compare today's landscapes with what he saw. And in all of Florida, there is no better site for that than Paynes Prairie State Preserve, a place Bartram described in detail.

In 1774, Bartram rode into a large basin in north-central Florida that he called the "great ALACHUA SAVANNA." He spent several days exploring the savanna, observing the land and the Indians that lived on it and the flora and fauna. So meticulous and inspiring were his writings that after the state of Florida acquired the savanna in the early 1970s, it established a goal "to restore, as nearly as possible, the conditions that existed on and around the basin during Bartram's visit." One thing it didn't restore was the name. By then, the great Alachua savanna had been renamed Paynes Prairie, after King Payne, a Seminole chief.

Unlike much of Florida, which is so sandy that it's hard to find a puddle after a hard rain, Paynes Prairie rests on a layer of water-impermeable clay. The rainwater that collects in the basin has only one way out, through Alachua Sink, a sinkhole near the northern rim of the prairie. But drainage is slow and imperfect, and summer rains flood the basin for several months each year. During prolonged dry spells, though, the marsh can become so parched that fires race across it. The combination of short, regular floods and occasional fires produces a type of freshwater marsh known as wet prairie, the most biologically diverse of all Florida marshes.

Diane and I arrive at Boulware Springs Park, the trailhead for Gainesville-Hawthorne Trail, on a warm, sunny day in early spring. In addition to my usual field guides, I have a copy of Bartram's *Travels* with me.

We follow Gainesville-Hawthorne Trail east along the northern rim of Paynes Prairie. It is an old road lined with live oaks and laurel oaks. Strands of silvery Spanish moss drip from huge limbs overhanging the road. Among the oaks stand a few longleaf pines, sweet gums, and magnolias—all trees that Bartram mentioned when he entered the prairie in 1774.

Farther down the road stands an oddball of a tree. It is an undistinguished thing thirty or forty feet tall with scraggly branches that are just beginning to leaf out. Despite its ordinary appearance at a distance, it is one of the easiest trees to identify up close. Its gray bark is covered with large, pyramid-shaped bumps, some of which are topped off by stiff thorns. Its name is Hercules-club, or *Zanthoxylum clava-herculis*, and if you cut out a three-foot section of its trunk, it would look just like the club a loincloth-clad Hercules would carry in a low-budget movie.

Bartram called this tree "Zanthoxylon clavis Herculis," but he probably also knew it by its common name, toothache tree. Hercules-club contains an alkaloid that acts as an anesthetic, and chewing the tree's bark or foliage relieves pain. Although remedies like this are only curiosities in these days of Novocaine and plentiful dentists, they were important in Bartram's time and afterward. As late as the turn of the century, Southern backwoodsmen were still using the sharp end of a rat-tail file to remove an aching tooth—a procedure that could make one want to chew bark.

Not far beyond the Hercules-club is La Chua Trail. We follow it down from the rim past huge oaks and sweet gums to the floor of the prairie. Horses graze in a nearby meadow, but a sign warning us not to get too close to the bison stops Diane in her tracks.

"Bison?" she says.

"They bother you?" I ask.

"Usually, you take me to places with really scary things, like ticks and mosquitoes. Compared to them, buffalo ought to be amusing. At least they won't eat me alive. Did Bartram really see buffalo in Florida?"

"Not exactly. A few were reintroduced here to make it *seem* more like Bartram's time."

In fact, when Bartram arrived in the South, the buffalo were gone, or nearly so. I dig *Travels* out of my pack and read aloud: " 'The buffalo (urus) once so very numerous, is not at this day to be seen in this part of the country.' But there *were* mosquitoes. Bartram says the Seminoles, who ran cattle on the prairie at the time of his visit, moved an entire town because of bad smells and 'the persecution of the mosquitoes.' "

We follow La Chua Trail south into a flat, nearly treeless basin. The ground beside the trail is dry, but marsh plants—cattail and smartweed and bright green maiden cane—grow nearby. To the east is Alachua Sink, the drain that keeps the basin from filling up with water—at least most of the time.

In the early 1870s, debris plugged Alachua Sink. Water rose in the basin, and the mostly dry savanna that Bartram had seen a hundred years earlier turned into a sixteen-thousand-acre lake deep enough for steamboats. In 1891, torrential rains apparently dislodged the plug. Within two weeks, the basin drained and the marsh began to re-form. Later, in the 1920s, dikes and canals were built to further dry the basin for cattle grazing. The result was the periodically flooded wet prairie that exists today.

The trail leads us to the edge of Alachua Sink. On the far side of the lake and in the canal that feeds it are alligators—small ones, medium-sized ones, and a few large ones. They sun themselves on the grassy banks and hang motionless in the still, black water. When we get too close, they slip sluggishly into deeper water, leaving scarcely a ripple.

Bartram saw alligators in this same spot more than two hundred years ago. Then, though, the gators were a bit larger and more numerous:

> In and about the Great Sink, are to be seen incredible numbers of crocodiles, some of which are of enormous size, and view the passenger with incredible impudence and avidity;

and at this time they are so abundant, that, if permitted by them, I could walk over any part of the bason and river upon their heads, which slowly float and turn about like knotty chunks or logs of wood, except when they plunge or shoot forward to beat off their associates, pressing too close to each other, or taking fish, which continually crowd in among them from the rivers and creeks draining from the savanna.

Walk across the lake on their heads? This passage has fascinated me since I first read it years ago. Did Bartram mean it literally? Could the lake have been that tightly packed with gators? Did they really eye him with "impudence and avidity"? I'm not the first naturalist to question Bartram's observations; speculations about their accuracy are a dime a dozen. In fact, *Travels* supports a minor industry. Countless scholarly articles have tried to figure out where Bartram went, what he saw, and when he saw it—and whether it was really possible that such and such was there. Almost without exception, they have concluded that if Bartram said he saw something, *he really did see it.*

A classic example is Bartram's discovery of the celestial lily. For years, no one could find such a plant, and some historians concluded they had caught him in an error. They used the missing lily to discredit some of his other observations. Then, in 1931, the celestial lily was rediscovered exactly as Bartram described it.

So when Bartram says that the gators at the sinkhole were so thick that he could have walked across the lake on their heads, I believe him. I can even imagine such a sight. But I still have a problem with the gators eying him with "impudence and avidity." I have been around a lot of alligators, and with one or two exceptions, they ignored me. Consequently, I tend to treat them a little cavalierly. Of course, as in the case of the missing lily, Bartram is probably right, and if I lose a leg to an impudent gator someday, I'll have nobody to blame but myself.

Beyond Alachua Sink, the trail meanders through waist-high marsh. Besides the easily recognized maiden cane and cattails, I spot patches of soft rush in wet areas and broom sedge in drier ones. Botanists have identified over seven hundred species of plants on the prairie, many of them grasses. There are spike grass, carpet grass, goose grass, finger grass, needlegrass, and two species of crab grass. But on the fecund, wet prairie, it is almost impossible for a nonspecialist to distinguish these species. Out here, they appear as a vast expanse of green, the different grasses locked together in a great amorphous mass.

Farther along, bright yellow tiger swallowtails catch a breeze and swirl down the path. Sparrows and grackles duck in and out of the reeds, and great blue herons stand immobile in patches of open water. Alligators are everywhere.

Suddenly, from behind a grove of trees near the rim, two ospreys shoot into sight, flapping mightily to gain altitude. Chasing them is a bald eagle. One of the ospreys disappears behind the trees, but the other one catches a thermal and soars upward, pursued closely by the eagle. Gradually, the distance between the two birds increases as they spiral higher into the blue sky. Finally, the osprey seems to know it's safe, and eagle and osprey circle companionably around one another until I lose sight of them. Both eagles and ospreys nest on Paynes Prairie, and I suspect the eagle was after them because the ospreys got too close to its nest, but for all I know, they were just playing or showing off.

Later, we spot a half-dozen ibises parading around a shallow pond, feeding and preening. In the center of the pond only a few feet from the ibises lies a six-foot-long gator. The birds ignore the gator, who returns the favor and ignores them.

At the end of La Chua Trail, wooden stairs lead us to the top of a low platform. For the first time, we get a bird's-eye view of the wet prairie. It is a patchwork of small ponds, muddy marshes, and dry ground. Hundreds of boat-tailed grackles fly back and forth from marsh to pond to ground, hopping around, calling to one another. Along the trail, the grackles were out of sight, and we became so accustomed to their repetitive croaks and whistles that their voices faded unnoticed into a background blur, like Muzak on an elevator. But from up here, each bird is visible and noisy.

Ibises, snowy egrets, and a black-crowned night heron stalk through the shallow waters of ponds below the tower. Red patches flash on dark wings as a swirl of red-winged blackbirds moves from one patch of marsh to another, then to yet another. Almost every pond has a resident gator. We glass the area for buffalo but see none.

After watching the show for a while, we leave the tower and retrace our footsteps, heading north on La Chua Trail. About halfway back, we stop to watch a dozen white lumps methodically eating their way across a dry, short-grass meadow. They are birds, stocky creatures with short yellow-green legs and stout yellow bills. Most of them are solid white, but a few have buff crowns and backs, their breeding colors. They are cattle egrets (*Bubulcus ibis*), birds that Bartram didn't mention because they weren't here at the time of his visit.

Dozens of species have been introduced at Paynes Prairie since Bartram passed through. Many of the common plants—hydrilla, Johnson grass, chickweed, and two species of morning glory—are imports. Most of them arrived as inadvertent offshoots of human travel, as hitchhikers in trouser cuffs or suitcases. Some introduced wildlife, like starlings and carp, spread across the country after being released deliberately by well-meaning men. But cattle egrets got here in an altogether different fashion: they came on their own.

The first cattle egrets in the New World appeared in Dutch Guiana (now Suriname) in 1877. Ornithologists believe they got there the hard way, by flying across the Atlantic Ocean from Africa, a distance of nearly eighteen hundred miles. Why the first egrets made that daunting voyage is open to question, but cows were probably the reason they stayed. Large-scale cattle ranching was just developing in the Americas, and cattle egrets, as their name implies, are usually found around cows (and other ungulates such as Cape buffalo, wildebeests, and zebras).

As cows feed, their hooves flush a bounty of insects, on which the egrets feast. Unlike starlings, carp, and crab grass, which competed with native species, cattle egrets did not displace other birds. They found an unoccupied ecological niche and filled it. The first cattle egrets in North America were spotted in Florida in 1941. By 1995, they had spread to most of the lower forty-eight states and several Canadian provinces. In Florida, they have become so plentiful that most people either don't notice them or assume they are farm pests. But these plucky little African egrets are actually the farmer's friend, munching down hundreds of crop-eating grasshoppers and crickets a day.

At the end of La Chua Trail, we run into a ranger, a tall young man with an intense mien. "See any alligators on the path?" he asks.

"Lots of gators," I reply, "but none on the path."

His face relaxes into a more cheerful expression. "Good. They get aggressive this time of year. My job is to run them off the trail."

"Also plenty of cattle egrets," Diane adds, "but no cattle and no buffalo. I really wanted to see buffalo."

"They're here," says the ranger, "but they're hard to find. The ticks and mosquitoes bother them real bad."

I pull out my copy of *Travels* again. "When Bartram passed through, he said the buffalo were gone from the South because they were 'affrighted away' by Europeans. We probably affrighted these."

"I doubt it," Diane says. "I bet the mosquitoes and ticks got them."

BEFORE YOU GO

For More Information
Paynes Prairie State Preserve
Route 2, Box 41
Micanopy, FL 32667
(352) 466-4100

Accommodations
The trailhead for Gainesville-Hawthorne State Trail is in Boulware Springs Park, on the northern rim of Paynes Prairie just south of Gainesville. The main entrance to the preserve is near the southern rim just north of Micanopy. Motels are available in both towns. For information, contact

Alachua County Visitors and Convention Bureau
30 East University Avenue
Gainesville, FL 32601
(352) 374-5231

Campgrounds
Paynes Prairie has a 50-site campground east of Lake Wauberg, near the southern entrance to the preserve.

Maps
The free leaflet *Paynes Prairie State Preserve* contains a trail map that is suitable for this walk.

Fees

If you walk into the preserve on
Gainesville-Hawthorne State Trail, admission is free. A fee of $3.25 per car
is charged at the southern entrance.

Points of Interest

Several trails start in the vicinity of Lake
Wauberg Recreation Area in the southern part of Paynes Prairie
State Preserve. Hikes along Cone's Dike and around Chacala Pond
take you through pine flatwoods and mixed forests as well as the
wet-prairie ecosystem.

Additional Reading

"African Egrets? Holy Cow!" by Les Line, *International Wildlife*
25, November–December 1995, 44–54.

John and William Bartram by Ernest Earnest, University of Pennsylvania Press, Philadelphia, 1940.

"Kubla Khan" by Samuel Taylor Coleridge, in *English Poetry*,
volume 2 of *The Harvard Classics*, P. F. Collier and Son, New York,
1910.

A Naturalist in Florida: A Celebration of Eden by Archie Carr,
edited by Marjorie Harris Carr, Yale University Press, New Haven, Connecticut, 1994.

Some Kind of Paradise: A Chronicle of Man and the Land in Florida
by Mark Derr, William Morrow and Company, New York, 1989.

Travels of William Bartram, Naturalist's Edition, by William Bartram, edited with commentary and an annotated index by Francis Harper, Yale University Press, New Haven, Connecticut, 1958. Billy Bartram was a fine writer and naturalist, but he wasn't good on dates. Many of the dates in *Travels* are wrong, sometimes by as much as a year. Bartram's spelling and nomenclature were also erratic. Although the Dover Publications edition of *Travels* is adequate for most purposes, scholarly research requires this volume. In it, Francis Harper's commentary gently corrects and clarifies *Travels* where necessary. The annotated index is a major improvement over other reprints.

Old Florida

North End Trails
Manatee Springs State Park

Manatee Springs State Park lies on the eastern bank of the Suwannee River 6 miles west of Chiefland on S.R. 320. The 2,075-acre park is named for a first-magnitude spring on the property, and the spring is named for the manatees that sometimes visit it.

Scenic Trail starts in a small parking lot just off Main Park Drive. The trail runs north through a mixed forest of pines and hardwoods to an intersection with Clay Road. Follow Clay Road east to Shacklefoot Trail. Proceed north on Shacklefoot to its intersection with Graveyard Trail, then east on Graveyard to a path that follows the park fence back to Shacklefoot. Take Shacklefoot Trail south to Main Park Drive. From there, it is 0.1 mile back to the trailhead.

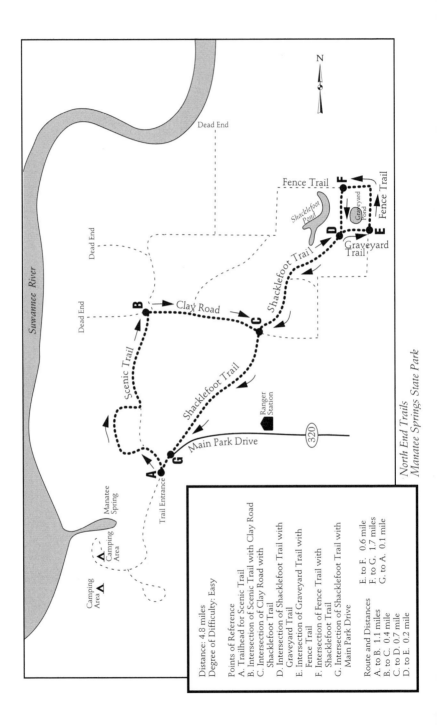

N

Dead End

Dead End

Dead End

Dead End

Suwannee River

Fence Trail

F

Fence Trail

Shacklefoot Pond

Graveyard Pond

D

E

Graveyard Trail

Shacklefoot Trail

B Clay Road **C**

Scenic Trail

Shacklefoot Trail

Ranger Station

320

A **G** Main Park Drive

Trail Entrance

Manatee Spring

Camping Area

Camping Area

Camping Area

North End Trails
Manatee Springs State Park

Distance: 4.8 miles
Degree of Difficulty: Easy

Points of Reference
A. Trailhead for Scenic Trail
B. Intersection of Scenic Trail with Clay Road
C. Intersection of Clay Road with
   Shacklefoot Trail
D. Intersection of Shacklefoot Trail with
   Graveyard Trail
E. Intersection of Graveyard Trail with
   Fence Trail
F. Intersection of Fence Trail with
   Shacklefoot Trail
G. Intersection of Shacklefoot Trail with
   Main Park Drive

Route and Distances
A. to B. 1.1 miles   E. to F. 0.6 mile
B. to C. 0.4 mile   F. to G. 1.7 miles
C. to D. 0.7 mile   G. to A. 0.1 mile
D. to E. 0.2 mile

Florida is made of limestone. The golf courses, condominiums, and freeways of modern Florida rest on ancient layers of calcium carbonate that precipitated out of the shallow seas that once covered the state and the remains of marine creatures that died in those seas. Calcium carbonate, however, dissolves in water, which makes the geology of this flat, seemingly monotonous land more interesting than one might think.

At Manatee Springs State Park, rainwater has seeped into the apparently solid earth and riddled it with underground fissures and caverns. When the limestone roof of a cavern erodes and collapses, you get a sinkhole. If water collects in the sinkhole, you get a sinkhole lake.

This Swiss-cheese topography (known to geologists as karst, for a similar region in Yugoslavia) also creates artesian springs. Manatee Springs is an example. From it gushes 117 million gallons of seventy-two-degree water a day. The green, pellucid stream flows down a short spring run to the Suwannee River and on to the Gulf of Mexico. Florida has twenty-seven first-magnitude springs (springs that discharge 4,500 gallons or more per minute), and they have long been magnets for wildlife and people.

Fish and turtles swim in the hospitable waters of Manatee Springs, which was named for the manatees that visit it. Hundreds of these huge "sea cows" have been sighted in the park in the last few years, but until recently, manatees were uncommon. They returned after hydrilla was cleared from the spring run and powerboats were banned. In 1995, a calf was born near the mouth of the spring run.

Other creatures also enjoy the spring. Birds soar overhead, and deer come to drink. Lured by the game, the Seminoles came here regularly. The spring also attracted people interested in flora and geology. William Bartram, one of the first naturalists to explore Florida, stopped by in 1774.

Bartram was enchanted by the spring, which he called "the product of primitive nature, not to be imitated, much less equalled, by the united effort of human power and ingenuity!" While exploring here, he found the skeleton of a manatee that the Indians had killed for food the previous winter. He also wrote a good description of the spring and rattled off the scientific names of the plants and trees surrounding it.

Bartram never used the term *Old Florida* in his writings about the state, but today's Floridians use it regularly, if wistfully. Old Florida is the Florida that Bartram described. It is a mythical place to many tourists and residents, a place people yearn for but believe is gone forever. However, thanks to the state's protection and management of natural areas, Old Florida exists, and one place you can find it is in the karstic landscape of Manatee Springs State Park.[1]

Scenic Trail begins half a mile north of Manatee Springs. It is a sandy road overhung by sprawling live oaks. The trees drip with Spanish moss, and resurrection ferns cover the oaks' broad limbs. The understory is a thicket of saw palmettos and wax myrtles. After a few hundred yards, the trail passes a cypress-rimmed pond. Today, the cypresses are just leafing out, and their needles are bright green with the first blush of photosynthesis.

Bartram described the same flora in places almost identical to this one, but he employed more florid language. A live oak "spreads abroad his brawny arms, to a great distance." Spanish moss "is a singular and surprising vegetable production . . . [that] spreads into short and intricate divarications." And the cypress's "majestic stature is surprising; and on approaching it, we are struck with a kind of awe."

Despite the romantic prose, it's easy to recognize that the country we are walking through today hasn't changed much since Bartram's time. It is beautiful country, definitely Old Florida, and as Diane and I proceed north on the trail on the first morning of spring, there's no place I'd rather be.

Beyond the slough, red maples and sweet gums replace the cypresses, and the dark green red bays in the understory are diminutive reflections of the leathery-leaved magnolias towering above them. A red-bellied woodpecker lights in a palmetto not

[1] The state parks call themselves "the *Real* Florida." For more about the distinction between "Old Florida" and "the *Real* Florida," see the previous chapter, "A Walk with Billy."

twenty feet from us, and the shrill *keee-o, keee-o* of a red-tailed hawk comes from deep in the woods. A few loblolly pines begin to show up among the hardwoods. We occasionally spot an odd-looking plant below the trees that appears to be a cross between a palm and a fern. It is Florida arrowroot, or coontie, *Zamia integrifolia*,[2] and it is, in fact, an oddball.

Coontie is a waist-high plant with stiff leaves that resemble the fronds of a large fern or small palm. It looks like the sago palm of Indonesia, which is sold in this country as an ornamental. Like

---

[2] Confusion surrounds the scientific name of this unassuming plant. For more information, refer to "More about Coontie" in the "Before You Go" section.

the sago palm, coontie has almost no visible stem or trunk, and its leaves grow from a woody crown that protrudes no more than a few inches above the ground. But unlike the sago palm, coontie isn't a palm at all, it is a cycad. Cycads are a two-hundred-million-year-old family of plants, most of whose members are now extinct. As with other survivors of ancient lines—coelacanths and sea turtles, for example—virtually every popular account of cycads refers to them as "living fossils."

Cycads are unbranched plants or trees that produce cones similar to ordinary pine cones. Pollen from male cones is carried by wind or insects to female cones, which yield seeds that sprout and become baby cycads. The only thing unusual about this is the cones themselves. Some cycads develop huge cones. The largest are those of an Australian cycad, *Lepidozomia peroffskyana*, which is only twenty feet tall but bears cones that can weigh one hundred pounds or more. Coontie cones are only four inches long—a little smaller than those produced by a hundred-foot longleaf pine, but not bad for a plant the size of an azalea.

As we continue north through the flatwoods, a warm breeze ruffles the fronds of saw palmettos. Tall cabbage palms and an occasional longleaf pine rise into the cloudless blue sky. A faint ashy scent permeates the air. Soon, charred tree trunks begin to appear beside the trail, and scrubby oaks dominate the understory. By the time we reach Clay Road, longleaf pines have become common.

Park manager Paul Perras regularly conducts controlled burns in this section of the park. His goal is to restore the longleaf-pine uplands that existed here before the pines were logged early in this century. The presence of longleaf pines in today's forest indicates that the burns are doing the job, but the thriving scrub oaks show that more fires will be needed to completely restore the original ecosystem. (See the chapter "A Forest Redux" for a more complete account of the effects of fire on longleaf-pine habitats.)

Deer tracks dimple the sand of Clay Road, and clumps of yucca mingle with coontie and bracken in the understory. Brightly colored dragonflies and butterflies flit among red bays, and tiny yellow flowers of oxalis brighten the margin of the old road.

At Shacklefoot Trail, we head north again. We follow Graveyard Trail east to Fence Trail, which loops back to Shacklefoot. From the trail, two ponds are visible. Shacklefoot Pond lies to the west and Graveyard Pond to the east. Shacklefoot is the larger of the two, which appear to be almost identical otherwise. But appearances are deceiving: Shacklefoot is a typical swamp pond, a low place where surface water collects, and Graveyard Pond is a sinkhole lake. Beneath its dark waters is a cavern of limestone.

Bartram was quite taken with these limestone sinks, where the waters "descend by slow degrees, through rocky caverns into the bowels of the earth." And one of his readers, the poet Samuel Taylor Coleridge, was quite taken with Bartram's descriptions of them. In fact, much of "Kubla Khan" was based on Bartram's writings about a sinkhole lake. (See the previous chapter, "A Walk with Billy," for more about the influence of Bartram on English poets.)

After passing the ponds, Shacklefoot continues south beneath live oaks and sweet gums. Yuccas reappear in the understory, and woodpeckers call from the woods. Near Clay Road, the country opens up again. Yellow and white wildflowers bloom under longleaf pines, which have replaced the hardwoods in the forest. The reason is summarized on a sign: "Burn History—6/87, 9/89, 3/93, 4/94."

Beyond the pines, near the end of the trail, live oaks dominate again, their sturdy branches closing in over the path. A red-tailed hawk, probably the one we heard when we started our walk, cries out from above the canopy. Patches of sunlight dapple the sandy road, and the hawk's shadow floats across the patches. A second hawk joins the one above us. The two swoop back and forth above the trees. Finally, I get a good look at one through a hole in the canopy. It spots me and banks sharply, its rufous tail agleam in the sunlight. The second hawk soars above it, then swoops toward us. Their aggressive behavior almost certainly means the hawks have a nest nearby. I scan the trees but can't locate it.

Red-tailed hawks (*Buteo jamaicensis*) are the largest hawks found in Florida. According to Arthur Cleveland Bent in *Life Histories of North American Birds of Prey*, they are not aggressive in defending their nests. "They seem to be more concerned about their own safety than about the welfare of their eggs or young," he wrote. Hawks, though—like other wildlife and humans—aren't manufactured, aren't stamped out with a DNA cookie cutter, and these two obviously haven't read Bent's book. As I watch, they sail ever lower over our heads, squealing at us, skimming the tops of the trees.

If some red-tailed hawks are less than pugnacious in defending their young, they are all aggressive in obtaining food for them. These hawks will bring home almost anything, from porcupines to squirrels, from owls to rattlesnakes to other hawks. One of Bent's correspondents described a hair-raising encounter between a red-tail and an oversized tomcat that ended in a draw. But my favorite story about red-tails comes from Bartram. A few days before he reached Manatee Springs, Bartram was riding ahead of his companions when an unusual scene unfolded:

> The high road being here open and spacious, at a good
> distance before me, I observed a large hawk on the ground in
> the middle of the road: he seemed to be in distress endeav-
> ouring to rise; when, coming up near him, I found him closely
> bound up by a very long coach-whip snake, that had wreathed
> himself several times around the hawk's body, who had but
> one of his wings at liberty: beholding their struggles a while, I
> alighted off my horse with an intention of parting them; when,
> on coming up, they mutually agreed to separate themselves. . . .
> The bird rose aloft and fled away as soon as he recovered his
> liberty, and the snake as eagerly made off.

Bartram never identified the hawk as a red-tail, but his description of it as a "large hawk" leads me to guess that it was. Besides,
coachwhips are active snakes that bite vigorously and can reach
seven feet in length, and I suspect that only a hawk known to eat
rattlesnakes and porcupines would have had the nerve to attack
one.

After we finish our walk, we drive to Manatee Springs. We saw
only two other hikers on the trails, but the picnic area and snack
bar at the spring are jammed with children and their parents.
One man is snorkeling in the clear, blue-green boil, and elderly
couples stroll around snapping pictures. Manatee Springs has long
been a gathering place for people, and it remains one today.

We walk out on the boardwalk that parallels the spring run
and follow it to the Suwannee River, wide and deep and black in
the afternoon sun. Tall cypresses mixed with ironwoods and river
birches grow in the bottom land beside the river. Schools of mullet

hang in the current in the clear water of the run, and turtles swim beside the boardwalk.

Though the run is packed with life, it hardly compares with what Bartram found here over two hundred years ago. "It is amazing," he wrote, "and almost incredible, what troops and bands of fish and other watery inhabitants are now in sight, all peaceable; and in what variety of gay colors and forms, continually ascending and descending, roving and figuring amongst one another, yet every tribe associating separately."

Long after Bartram's visit, another fine naturalist spent time at Manatee Springs. Archie Carr, the famous herpetologist from the University of Florida, dedicated much of his life to studying and trying to save sea turtles. But long before he got interested in those charismatic creatures, he came here to investigate another turtle, the far less glamorous big-headed stinkjim.

Carr first visited Manatee Springs in 1935, twenty years before it became a state park. No fish and little marine life of any kind were in the spring at the time, and Carr attributed the absence to dynamiters.

One of the dynamiters who frequented Manatee Springs was an old-timer named John Henry. Carr knew him well and attested to his skill with the explosive. John Henry, Carr said admiringly, "could get that [a stick of dynamite] out into a nervous school of big, cruising mullet in an arc so well timed that it would go off as it hit and blow the fish out of the water before they could shy at the splash."

Since those days, big changes have occurred. Manatee Springs is now a state park, logging is prohibited, the dynamiters are gone, and the mullet are back in the spring run. If the fish are not as plentiful now as they were in Bartram's day, they are certainly more numerous than they were when Carr first visited.

Like the mullet, the upland-pine ecosystem is coming back, and the flatwoods are healthy. In fact, if you ignore the crowds at the spring, the country more closely resembles the place Bartram described over two hundred years ago than the one Archie Carr knew. Yes, Old Florida can be found at Manatee Springs. And I'm sure that Professor Carr, who devoted his professional life to wildlife conservation, would approve of the changes that have brought it back—though he might miss John Henry a little.

BEFORE YOU GO

For More Information
    Manatee Springs State Park
    11650 Northwest 115th Street
    Chiefland, FL 32626
    (352) 493-6072

Accommodations
    The nearest town is Chiefland, about 6 miles east of the park. For information, contact

    Chiefland Chamber of Commerce
    P.O. Box 1397
    Chiefland, FL 32644
    (352) 493-1849

Campgrounds

Campers have their choice of 86 sites in the park campground.

Maps

The free "North End Trail Map" available from the ranger station at the park's entrance is all you will need to navigate these well-marked trails.

Fees

Admission to the park is $3.25 per car.

More about Coontie

The first plant of the genus *Zamia* was described in 1659. It was *Z. pumila*, a coontie variant found in Cuba, Puerto Rico, and the Dominican Republic. The Florida version of coontie was so similar that early botanists (including William Bartram) referred to it as *Z. pumila*. To further confuse the matter, some later scientists (including Archie Carr) recognized another coontie variant, *Z. floridana*, as a separate species. These days, most botanists believe that there is only one species of Florida coontie, and they have named it *Z. integrifolia*.

Points of Interest

After a walk on the North End trails, a canoe trip down the short spring run to the Suwannee River is a good way to explore Manatee Springs. When you reach the river, head upstream for as far as your arms and shoulders are willing, then ride the current back down. During our trip, fish and turtles swam languidly beside our canoe while vultures and raptors soared overhead. We didn't encounter any manatees, but we could have.

Canoes may be rented at the park's snack bar for a small fee.

Additional Reading

Cycads of the World by David L. Jones, Smithsonian Institution Press, Washington, 1993.

Life Histories of North American Birds of Prey, part 1, by Arthur Cleveland Bent, Dover Publications, New York, 1961. This book was originally published in 1937 as the Smithsonian Institution's *Bulletin 167*.

A Naturalist in Florida: A Celebration of Eden by Archie Carr, edited by Marjorie Harris Carr, Yale University Press, New Haven, Connecticut, 1994.

Travels of William Bartram by William Bartram, edited by Mark Van Doren, Dover Publications, New York, 1955. This book was originally published in Philadelphia in 1791 under the title *Travels through North & South Carolina, Georgia, East & West Florida, the Cherokee Country, the Extensive Territories of the Muscogulges, or Creek Confederacy, and the Country of the Chactaws*.

Ecology 101

Nature and Hiking Trails
Little Talbot Island State Park

Little Talbot is a 5-mile-long barrier island located on S.R. A1A between Amelia Island and Jacksonville. All of the island's 2,500 acres are in the state park.

This walk begins at a small parking lot a few yards from the ranger station, just northeast of A1A. The park's two trails form a connected double loop. From the ranger station, follow the entrance road across A1A and through the campground. The Nature Trail, a 1-mile loop, starts at the southern tip of the campground near campsite 39. After finishing it, head back across A1A. The trailhead for the Hiking Trail is on the entrance road between the highway and the ranger station. Follow the sandy path through a maritime forest and complete the 4.1-mile loop by returning along the beach to the ranger station.

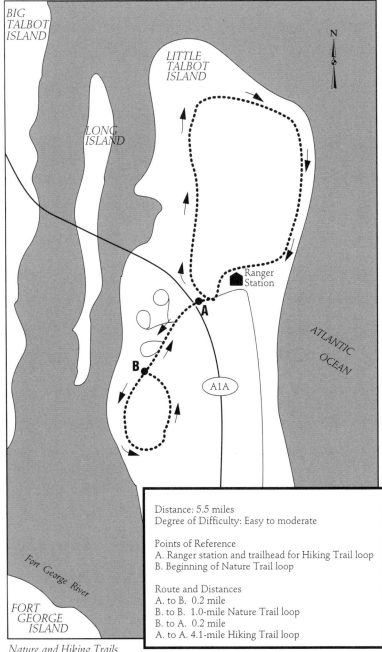

BIG TALBOT ISLAND

LITTLE TALBOT ISLAND

N

LONG ISLAND

Ranger Station

ATLANTIC OCEAN

A

B

A1A

Fort George River

FORT GEORGE ISLAND

Distance: 5.5 miles
Degree of Difficulty: Easy to moderate

Points of Reference
A. Ranger station and trailhead for Hiking Trail loop
B. Beginning of Nature Trail loop

Route and Distances
A. to B. 0.2 mile
B. to B. 1.0-mile Nature Trail loop
B. to A. 0.2 mile
A. to A. 4.1-mile Hiking Trail loop

Nature and Hiking Trails
Little Talbot Island State Park

■

Little Talbot is one of the few never-developed barrier islands on Florida's Atlantic coast. It is a drumstick-shaped patch of land lying between Nassau Sound and the mouth of the St. John's River. It was formed by longshore currents that deposited sand on the seaward side of the island in long, parallel ridges, a process that is still under way. Consequently, the oldest part of the island is its western edge, and the land nearest the ocean is the newest. On Little Talbot, as on other barrier islands, the age of the land and its distance from the sea strongly influence the nature of its ecosystems.

Although life originated in the ocean, most earth-based plants and animals find the sea a harsh mother. Shifting sands and wind-driven salt spray, storms and the steady pounding of surf make life tenuous. To survive near the sea, terrestrial plants and animals must—with one exception we will get to later—acknowledge its overwhelming force and hunker down. This walk, from a live-oak hammock on the western side of the island to the raw sand of the beach, passes through three ecological zones and illustrates how proximity to the sea affects life on a barrier island.

I walk west from the ranger station on a warm, overcast day in early spring. A sandy road leads into a nearly deserted campground. Tall palmettos, slash pines, and huge, dark green cedars line the road. Beneath them are wax myrtles, red bays, and a thicket of coral honeysuckle, a native plant with pink, trumpetlike flowers. A butterfly, a copper-colored Gulf fritillary, sips nectar from tiny yellow flowers.

The road continues west across rows of ancient sand dunes separated from one another by swales. Deeper in the campground, where the Nature Trail starts, live oaks replace cedars as the dominant trees, and their great branches, festooned with Spanish moss, overhang the road. The Nature Trail leads to a salt marsh—land's end. Inland from the marsh, the oaks and palmettos are tall and thick, even defiant. Here, on the oldest part of the island, the restless sea is a distant memory.

Coral beans bloom bright red beneath a dense understory of wax myrtles. Raccoon tracks dimple the sand beside them. This is perfect coon country, with big trees and their inevitable hollows to serve as dens, a salt marsh to provide aquatic appetizers, and a campground to supply the entrées.

But raccoons don't really need ideal habitat. The species is found throughout Florida and the continental United States. Raccoons flourish in places that most wildlife can't tolerate, like campgrounds and suburbs and even cities. I once

glimpsed two raccoons in my backyard in the middle of San Francisco and found an overturned garbage can the next morning to confirm it. *Procyon lotor* is a very adaptable animal indeed.

One place raccoons haven't adapted to is the beach and its adjacent dunes. They need fresh water to drink and sizable trees for their dens, so they tend to avoid the seashore—except for nighttime forays to search for turtle eggs and crabs.

One reason raccoons are so adaptable is their diet; coons will eat almost anything. Audubon, who kept a pet raccoon, noted, "It was truly omnivorous: never refusing anything eatable, vegetable or animal, cooked or uncooked, all was devoured with equal avidity." He didn't mention Chinese takeout, but I know raccoons love leftover Szechuan shrimp and lo mein, especially when served in a San Francisco trash can.

The trail soon turns east, away from the marsh. The cedars in this part of the forest are enormous, with gnarly limbs that resemble live oaks. Saw palmettos appear in the understory, and slash pines become more abundant. The path is soft and comforting, the walking easy.

Minutes later, I finish the Nature Trail, backtrack through the campground, and begin the Hiking Trail. The country here is more open, but the vegetation is similar to that of the hammock: live oaks and cedars, red bays and wax myrtles. Occasionally, the trail crosses desertlike patches of fine white sand. The land here is newer than that of the hammock, the soil less well developed.

I proceed north into the heart of the island, into the backdune ecosystem. Gradually, the more salt-tolerant cedars begin to

supplant live oaks as the dominant trees. Low-lying scrub oaks appear in the forest, with yaupons as understory. Slash pines also grow here, but they are scarcer than in the live-oak hammock. Purple spiderworts bloom beside the path, and tracts of bare sand now regularly interrupt the forest.

Some creatures like the open terrain, and the songs of cardinals and Carolina wrens accompany me on the trail. A spectacular summer tanager sits in an oak, a rosy blob among dull green leaves. A lizard scoots along the trunk of a long-dead sun-bleached tree. Actually, it is only part of a lizard; it has a stump where its tail used to be. The lizard pauses long enough for me to identify it as a Southeastern five-lined skink, *Eumeces inexpectatus*, a fast-moving, four-inch-long, yellow-striped brown streak that usually sports a long blue tail.

These skinks are found throughout Florida and the Southern

coastal plain as far north as Virginia. They are well adapted to the sandy, dry conditions of the back dunes. To conserve water, terrestrial reptiles such as skinks don't urinate. They excrete nitrogenous wastes in the form of solid or semisolid uric acid. Thus, unlike raccoons, skinks require very little fresh water. Nor do they need large dens in which to sleep and raise their young; skinks can spend their nights beneath a rock and lay their eggs in rotting wood. And when storms roar in from the ocean, they simply lie low. Being cold-blooded, skinks can endure long periods of inactivity without eating, a luxury no active mammal can afford.

But being a reptile has its disadvantages. Cool, overcast weather slows a skink down. If a raccoon should happen upon it on such a day, the skink could easily lose its long, brilliant blue tail. Skinks are autotomic, so the tail will grow back, but if it should bump into another raccoon before it does, it might lose something irreplaceable.

The trail continues north, then curls east. For the first time today, I hear the low rumble of surf. The forest flattens out into wax-myrtle scrub, and white dunes rise in the distance. The only trees are dwarfs: twisted cedars, tattered palmettos. As I approach the beach, even those vanish. Only the sea oats stand upright on the foredunes; the rest of the vegetation—pennywort, primrose, and smilax—hugs the sand to avoid wind and salt spray.

The trail leads to the top of the dunes. Before me is bare beach, the last of Little Talbot's ecological zones. I scramble down to the sea.

The warm day has become warmer, but breeze cools the shore, bringing with it the tangy smell of open sea. The beach is deserted, and the hard-packed sand is a pleasant change from the soft white sugar of the dunes. Laughing gulls sail overhead, and three black skimmers fly low, dipping their beaks into the backwash of waves. Sanderlings race back and forth on the beach, bobbing their heads as they probe the moist sand just beyond the reach of the surf.

The broken remains of angel wings, cockles, and arks lie on the beach. No land animals live here, and the only vegetation is washed-up strands of seaweed. Life is plentiful, though, even in the seemingly inhospitable intertidal zone. But it's even more prostrate than in the dunes; to find it, you must dig into the moist beach.

Tiny crabs and shrimps and worms live just beneath the surface of the sand. These are the creatures on which the sanderlings are feeding. But larger animals lurk below them. Telltale keyholes mark the presence of clams, and the sandy tunnels that riddle the upper beach lead to the hiding places of ghost crabs. Bristly, foot-long lugworms lie buried beneath the low-tide line, and millions of coquinas filter diatoms from the sand-and-sea slurry of the intertidal zone.

Farther down the beach, I spot a curious set of star-shaped sand ridges about a quarter of an inch high and eight inches across. I dig into the wet sand with my fingers and unearth a live starfish. When I wash the sand off, a beautiful creature emerges. It is mostly purple, with the margins of each arm outlined in delicate orange. My field guide tells me it is a plated-margined sea star, *Astropecten articulatus*, the first one I've ever seen.

Sea stars are members of the epibenthos, which are the flora and fauna found on the ocean floor between the low-tide line and the deep sea. Live specimens regularly wash ashore, and this species seems very much at home in the sand.

Like all sea stars, *A. articulatus* is carnivorous, preying on snails and sand dollars. A Northern relative, *Asterias forbesi*, or Forbes' common sea star, feeds on oysters and clams, prying open the valves and everting its stomach into the opening. The sea star then literally eats the shellfish alive. For an animal that can move only a few inches a minute, *A. forbesi* does real damage to shellfish beds, consuming half a dozen or so oysters a day. Naturally, oystermen don't care much for them. In Chesapeake Bay, they used to cut up sea stars and throw the remains overboard. It wasn't an effective means of population control. Sea stars, like skinks, are autotomic—except more so. They have amazing powers of re-generation, quickly growing a new arm when one is amputated and, in some species, growing a new star from the severed arm.

My book does not say precisely how *A. articulatus* goes about devouring its chosen prey of snails and sand dollars, but based on *A. forbesi's messiness* with oysters, what I imagine is so gruesome that I quickly lay the sea star back on the sand. It promptly bur-rows in, and three minutes later, all that's left is the same pattern of sandy ridges that originally attracted my attention.

Near the end of the walk, a gray hulk lies on the beach just above the wrack of the high-tide line. It is the remains of a log-gerhead turtle.

Loggerhead turtles, *Caretta caretta*, nest on the beach at Little Talbot. They—along with sea snakes and seals, whales and dol-phins—represent the pinnacle of terrestrial animals' adaptation to the sea. They are as much at home in salt water as sea stars—which never left it. Although hunkering down is the best strategy for surviving near the sea, once you take the plunge, the rules change.

Exactly how turtles evolved from the tetrapods that crawled out of the ocean 360 million years ago to colonize the land is not known; there is a 100-million-year gap in the fossil record. The first creature that was recognizably a turtle showed up about 200 million years ago, and they've been going strong ever since. Along with the crocodilians, turtles are the oldest land vertebrates still around.

Turtles evolved on land, but those that returned to the sea developed special equipment. Their feet turned into flippers; they lost the ability to withdraw into their shells; and they got bigger. Loggerheads of up to a thousand pounds were reported in the past, and the leatherback, our largest turtle, can reach fifteen hundred pounds. This combination of mobility in the water, tough shells, and large size makes sea turtles safe from most predators— but not all.

Aside from man, the loggerheads' most dangerous predator is . . . the raccoon. Coons love to eat the leathery, golf-ball-sized turtle eggs, and they exhibit an uncanny knack for sniffing them out. One study in the early 1980s showed that, south of here, in Canaveral National Seashore, raccoons destroyed almost every loggerhead nest in the park. To save sea-turtle eggs from raccoons, biologists have tried a number of tactics, from protecting nests with wire fences to digging up the eggs and incubating them indoors. They've also deported marauding coons inland, away from the beaches where turtles nest.

All of these methods work; as bright as coons are, we humans can easily outsmart them. Still, northern loggerhead populations (turtles that nest north of Jacksonville) continue to decline.

I walk around the dead turtle. It is over three feet long. White barnacles cling to its dull brown carapace. I see no injuries, no signs of violence. What could do in a creature this size? It may have died of old age and washed ashore. More likely, though, it was caught in a shrimper's trawl and drowned. In a 1990 report, the National Research Council stated flatly that "of all the known factors, by far the most important source of [sea turtle] deaths was the incidental capture of turtles (especially loggerheads and Kemp's ridleys) in shrimp trawling."

Federal regulations now require that shrimping trawls be out-fitted with turtle-excluder devices (TEDs). While these devices are effective, they are not perfect. This turtle could have been a victim of faulty design. Researchers are working to improve the performance of TEDs, and I believe they will succeed. We are the most intelligent species, the exception to the ecological rules. We don't have to hunker down to survive in Little Talbot's eco-systems, and we can go faster and farther than loggerheads in the open sea. Any species that can do all that, and outsmart raccoons to boot, can certainly design a shrimp net that will exclude sea turtles—all sea turtles.

BEFORE YOU GO

For More Information
Little Talbot Island State Park
12157 Heckscher Drive
Jacksonville, FL 32226
(904) 251-2320

Accommodations

The closest lodgings are on Amelia Island, about 17 miles north of Little Talbot Island State Park. Hotels, motels, and rental units are available. Contact

The Chamber
P.O. Box 472
Fernandina Beach, FL 32035-0472
(800) 226-3542

Campgrounds

Little Talbot Island State Park's 40 campsites are nestled under live oaks and cedars just west of S.R. A1A. It is a lovely campground, and the perfect place to start this walk. For more information, contact the park.

Maps

The free brochure *Little Talbot Island State Park* has a map of the Hiking Trail and the Nature Trail. Another free brochure, *Campground Nature Trail*, contains a more detailed map of the Nature Trail. Together, the two maps are adequate for these easy-to-follow trails.

Fees

The park charges a $3.25 entrance fee per car.

Points of Interest

Fort George Island State Cultural Site lies just south of Little Talbot Island. A 4.4-mile loop road called Saturiwa Trail takes the visitor past numbered signs that—when used with the key in an accompanying free booklet—illustrate the island's long history. The

Spaniards who arrived here in 1562 were greeted by Indians whose ancestors had lived on the island for 5,000 years. Not much remains of the early Spanish period, but the Indians' huge shell middens are still visible.

Since the earliest days of Europeans on Fort George, the island has followed a predictable path. First there was a mission, then a fort, a plantation, a private club, and finally developers. Today, the cultural site shares the island with privately owned homes.

The road around Fort George Island is shaded by pines and palmettos and live oaks. Visitors can walk, bicycle, or drive the loop. Several short walking paths start on the road and lead to historical sites.

Additional Reading

Audubon's Quadrupeds of North America, Wellfleet Press, Secaucus, New Jersey, 1989. This book is a revised edition of *Viviparous Quadrupeds of North America* by John James Audubon, which was originally published in 1842.

"The Chelonian Story" by Robert Reisz, *The Sciences*, July–August 1992, 37–43.

Decline of the Sea Turtles by National Research Council, National Academy Press, Washington, 1990.

"Florida's Marine Turtles" by David Arnold, *Florida Wildlife* 49, July–August 1995, 12–15.

"Natural History: Raccoon" by Linda Renshaw, *South Carolina Wildlife* 39, September–October 1992, 6–10.

A Sierra Club Naturalist's Guide to the Middle Atlantic Coast by Bill Perry, Sierra Club Books, San Francisco, 1985.

So Excellent a Fishe by Archie Carr, Natural History Press, New York, 1967. There's no better way to learn about sea turtles than by reading this book, written by a man who spent much of his life studying them.

The Year of the Turtle by David M. Carroll, Camden House Publishing, Charlotte, Vermont, 1991.

Songs of the River

Big Oak and Florida Trails
Suwannee River State Park

Suwannee River State Park's 1,856 acres lie at the confluence of the Suwannee and Withlacoochee Rivers, 13 miles west of Live Oak. The park office and campground are on the eastern bank of the Suwannee, but this walk is on the western side, on a peninsula bordered by the two rivers. There are no bridges across either river in the park.

To reach the trailhead, you must leave the park and drive northwest on U.S. 90 for 1.5 miles. After crossing the Suwannee River (at this point merged with the Withlacoochee), take a right on a paved road and an immediate left on an unnamed dirt road, which runs north for 1.5 miles and dead-ends at another paved road. A right turn takes you across the Withlacoochee. Another right turn at the end of the bridge puts you on a grassy road that leads to a gate with signs for Florida National Scenic Trail and the state park. This is private property, so don't block the driveway or the gate when you park. The walk begins at the gate.

An old road follows a gas-pipeline right of way for 200 yards to the park boundary and Big Oak Trail. Big Oak Trail runs west to the Withlacoochee, then parallels the river. At the tip of the peninsula, where the

(CONTINUED NEXT PAGE)

Withlacoochee and Suwannee meet, are a primitive camping area and an overlook offering good views of both rivers.

From the camping area, Big Oak Trail turns north, then east, paralleling the Suwannee and passing through a mature forest of oaks and pines. About halfway back, the trail leaves the Suwannee and heads due north to an intersection with Florida National Scenic Trail, which runs west back to the trailhead.

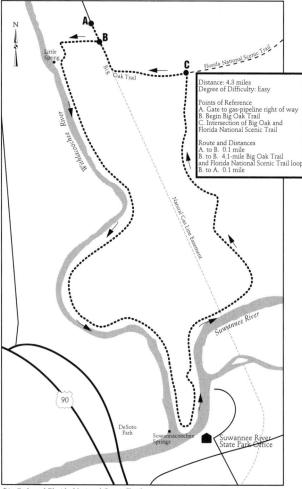

Distance: 4.3 miles
Degree of Difficulty: Easy

Points of Reference
A. Gate to gas-pipeline right of way
B. Begin Big Oak Trail
C. Intersection of Big Oak and
Florida National Scenic Trail

Route and Distances
A. to B. 0.1 mile
B. to B. 4.1-mile Big Oak Trail
and Florida National Scenic Trail loop
B. to A. 0.1 mile

Big Oak and Florida National Scenic Trails
Suwannee River State Park

The Suwannee River is famous throughout the United States, but except for some Floridians, almost nobody knows much about it. Few people know that the Suwannee is second in length only to the Apalachicola among Florida's rivers. Or that it rises in the Okefenokee Swamp in Georgia and flows for over two hundred miles across northern Florida before emptying into the Gulf of Mexico at Cedar Key. Most people haven't seen the Suwannee's meandering watercourse, bordered by tall cypresses and fed by the clear waters of numerous springs, or know that it is a wonderful river for canoeing, fishing, and wildlife watching. No, the Suwannee isn't famous because of its length or beauty or recreational possibilities. In fact, the river's celebrity is due to a song by a Pennsylvanian who never saw it.

How does one create a lasting song, a great painting, a literary masterpiece? If it could be explained, musicians, artists, and writers would crank out one great work after another. There is mystery in art, something deep and unfathomable that touches us. People who can create it better than others are called "talented," and by almost any measure, Stephen Foster was that.

With no formal training in music, Foster wrote over two hundred songs, some of which became musical staples. Whenever people gather around a piano, you are likely to hear "My Old Kentucky Home," "Camptown Races," "Beautiful Dreamer," or "Jeannie with the Light Brown Hair," all written by Foster nearly 150 years ago. Of course, everybody doesn't appreciate Stephen Foster songs. "Sentimental drivel," they sniff. But sentimental drivel or not, few people can look at the Suwannee River and not think of the opening lines of one of Foster's best-known songs, "Old Folks at Home":

> Way down upon the Swanee ribber,
> Far, far away,
> Dere's wha my heart is turning ebber,
> Dere's wha de old folks stay.

In 1852, a year after he wrote "Old Folks at Home," Foster made his only trip to the South. He took a steamboat to New Orleans from his home in Pittsburgh, and according to his brother Morrison Foster, that was as close as he ever came to the Suwannee River.

Stephen Foster died twelve years later at the American Hotel in New York City at the age of thirty-eight. He spent the last years of his life deep in debt and whiskey. At his funeral, a band of volunteer musicians played some of Foster's best-known songs, including "Old Folks at Home."

Diane and I start the grassy road that leads into Suwannee River State Park on a warm, overcast morning in early fall. Fire-ant

mounds line the old track, and butterflies sip nectar from wild-flowers along its margins. Low woods loom on both sides of the road. When we reach Big Oak Trail, we follow it west to the Withlacoochee River, then turn south and parallel it.

Limestone bluffs rise on both sides of the river, and a white-sand bottom is visible beneath the clear bottle-green water. Below the bluffs, along the riverbanks, moss-heavy cypresses and live oaks lean toward the water, angling for sunlight.

The trail passes through a dense second- or third-growth forest of maples, hollies, water oaks, and sweet gums. Beneath them is catbrier entangled in thickets of saw palmettos and yaupons. Deer tracks crisscross the sandy path.

This is good deer habitat: there's a river for drinking, understory for browsing, and nearby farms for serious chowing down. In fact, there are almost certainly more deer here today than there were over four centuries ago, when the Suwannee was called "the River of the Deer."

The name came from the first Europeans to see this part of Florida, Hernando De Soto and his gold-seeking band of adventurers. The party landed near Tampa Bay (De Soto scholars are still quibbling about the exact spot) on May 30, 1539. Within hours, a scouting party was set upon by six Indians "who tried to oppose him [the captain of the group] with their arrows." The party killed two of the Indians and soon began cutting down the "vast and lofty forest" into which the luckier Indians had escaped.

De Soto pushed inland from the bay and turned north, wreaking havoc on the Indians as he marched. After laying waste to the town of Napetaca, where "thirty or forty Indians were lanced," the party spent the night of September 23 beside the Suwannee near its junction with the Withlacoochee, about a mile from where we are now. Two Indians—probably having heard of De Soto's violent ways—brought him a stag as a gift. De Soto's men promptly named the waterway "the River of the Deer."

The trail continues south past sinkholes the size of bomb craters. Big carp drift by in the shallows of the river, and mullet splash noisily on the far side. Carolina wrens call from the brush. The forest is thick and shady, but occasional patches of longleaf pines and wire grass hint at the savanna that probably existed here before the region was logged.

After passing through another mile or so of second-growth forest, we arrive at the tip of the land. A high bluff overlooks the two rivers. The Withlacoochee, green and fast-flowing, is to our right, the tea-brown Suwannee to the left. The merged river is straight ahead, a dark, powerful stream. De Soto's men built a bridge across the Suwannee near this spot. A member of the expedition said the bridge was "three large pines in length and four in breadth," adding that "these pines were perfect and like the very large ones from Spain."

Pines that size no longer exist here; the few longleaf pines left are small trees. What happened to the "vast and lofty forest" that de Soto passed through on the way to his death beside the Mississippi River? The answer lies on the far side of the Withlacoochee. It's woods now, but the town of Ellaville once flourished there. It had several hundred residents, four sawmills, and seven turpentine stills.

Today, a historical marker stands where brawling loggers once drank together and argued prices. The sign tells of the town's glory days and ends this way: "Ellaville flourished as long as the yellow pine lasted. It declined after 1900 and ceased to exist when the post office closed in 1942." The sawmills and stills of Ellaville simply used up the resource that supported them.

It's not clear when or where the idea of sustained-yield forestry originated. Surely, fuel-poor Europeans understood and practiced some form of it long before they sent settlers to North America. But those settlers quickly forgot the concept when they disembarked in a vast land covered with virgin forests. They needed farmland, and trees were nuisance first and resource second.

Although Northern lands were heavily logged in the eighteenth century, large-scale logging in the South didn't begin until after the Civil War. The repeal of the Southern Homestead Law allowed the federal government to sell huge parcels of publicly owned land for $1.25 an acre. Cut-and-run loggers bought huge tracts of virgin forest, and towns like Ellaville sprouted like weeds in a garden to accommodate them. By the time Gifford Pinchot, the founder of the National Forest Service, introduced scientific forestry—and the idea of sustainable yields—to the country, it was too late for Ellaville. By 1901, loggers had so denuded the region that there weren't enough trees left to feed the town's insatiable sawmills.

The problem wasn't confined to northern Florida. That same year, Pinchot's friend President Teddy Roosevelt proclaimed, "The forest and water problems are perhaps the most vital internal problems of the United States. The fundamental idea of forestry is in the perpetuation of forests by use."

From the tip of the peninsula, Big Oak Trail turns north and parallels the Suwannee. It enters a dense grove of ironwoods with brown, muscular trunks, interspersed with a smattering of sparkleberries with peeling red bark. The trunks of both trees invite touching, and I hold out my hand to brush them as we walk by.

Farther along, the path veers inland, away from the white bluffs of the tree-lined Suwannee. Huge trees—live oaks, river birches, and loblolly pines—begin to appear in the forest, towering over the ironwoods and sparkleberries. Did the loggers of Ellaville, who once built a train trestle across the Withlacoochee to haul out the timber from this side of the river, miss this forest? Or did they cut it so long ago that it has recovered? No one knows for sure. I suspect they took the mature longleaf pines but spared the hardwoods and smaller pines.

In the darkest part of the forest, beneath towering spruce pines and sprawling live oaks, the understory trees vanish. Here, only low-lying saw palmettos grow beneath the gray Spanish moss that hangs from the dark green oaks. The parklike appearance of this spot—so different from anything else along the trail—is characteristic of old-growth forests. Perhaps no longleaf pines ever grew here, so this patch of land was never logged. In any case, the landscape appeals to me; I feel at home.

We take a break, sitting on a rotten log, swigging water and munching peanut-butter crackers. The semisweet odor of decay and rebirth rises from the black earth. It is a comforting place to rest.

Wilderness—a place where the hand of man is not evident, or only barely so—has that effect on some people. But unlike the easy-to-understand idea of sustainability, so eloquently spelled out by Pinchot and Roosevelt, the value of wilderness is difficult to articulate. Sustainability is an economic concept: act one way and you will use up the resource and wind up like Ellaville, act another way and it will last forever (or at least a very long time). Wilderness, though, has little to do with economics. Some people value it enormously, others not at all.

"We need the tonic of wildness," Thoreau said. It is fitting that our country's first wilderness proponent was a bit of a mystic, because the idea of conserving wilderness is mystical. Some scientists espouse the wilderness cause, pointing out that undisturbed areas serve as laboratories that enable them to study how ecosystems function. But most of the push for wilderness areas comes from those who feel a need for them and believe they are, in fact, a tonic.

In defending wilderness, science must give way to art. Why do we need wilderness? Why do we need Stephen Foster's songs? For many of us, they feed the soul, and we feel incomplete without them. The same mysterious process of creation went into both. The thought of living without songs or wilderness is unthinkable—but also unexplainable.

After our break, we begin walking north again. We pass a gigantic live oak that must be twenty feet around. This has to be the tree for which Big Oak Trail is named. Beyond it, though, the forest thins out, the trees shrink, the understory grows taller. Tangles of vines replace the saw palmettos. We are back into second-growth forest.

So close are the trees to the path that spiders have built webs across it. Some are nearly invisible, and I walk through them. After fifteen minutes of picking silvery filaments off my face, I ask Diane if she'd like to lead the way, but she's seen me clawing at my head and de- clines. Clearly, no one else has walked this trail today. By now, the morning overcast has cleared; shafts of sunlight penetrate the canopy and spotlight the forest floor. I see that the spiders have not confined their activities to the trail; in fact, al- most every ray of sunlight illuminates a spider web. Each web is different in size and shape and internal construction. Some are small and simple, consisting of only a few hori- zontal strands inches above the forest floor. Others are the complicated webs of orb weavers, intricate spiral constructions with heavy white cross-stitching near their centers.

Most of the spiders I spot are small, drab creatures, but near the end of the walk, I come within an inch or two of bumping into an exception that hangs from a web across the trail. The spider is level with my eyes. It's only a half-inch long, but compared to the other spiders I've glimpsed, it is positively garish. Its yellow body is shaped like a crab's and freckled with brown spots. Red spines rim its abdomen. If it has a head or legs, I can't identify them.

"Whoa," I call to Diane. "Take a look at this."

I flip through my field guide and there it is, on the last page. "Crablike spiny orb weaver," I say proudly. "*Gasteracantha elipsoides.*"

"Are you sure?" she asks. "It doesn't look like an orb weaver."

She's right, it doesn't. Most orb weavers—garden spiders and argiopes, for example—are normal-looking spiders with long legs and recognizable heads. What quirks of evolution formed this odd, colorful creature? To me, this spider is beautiful, as much a work of art as a great song or a wilderness.

I double-check my field guide and hand it to Diane. "Here it is," I say, pointing to the picture. "A work of art, a masterpiece of evolution."

Diane shuts the book and examines the spider. "Doesn't look like a masterpiece to me," she says. "It looks more like a tiny yellow crab than the *Mona Lisa*."

"But in its own way, it's just as lovely."

"Sure. All it lacks is a head and an enigmatic smile," she says, ducking under the web and heading for the car.

I take a last peek at the spider. That's another thing about art: everyone doesn't agree on what's a masterpiece. Some people don't even like "Old Folks at Home."

BEFORE YOU GO

For More Information
Suwannee River State Park
20185 County Road 132
Live Oak, FL 32060
(904) 362-2746

Accommodations

The closest town with motels is Lake City, about 30 miles southwest of the park. Contact

Lake City–Columbia County Chamber of Commerce
15 East Orange Street
Lake City, FL 32055
(904) 752-3690

Campgrounds

Suwannee River State Park has 31 campsites nestled under the pines and live oaks on the eastern side of the Suwannee River near the park office.

Maps

The excellent "Suwannee River State Park Trail Map," available at no charge from the park office, is suitable for this walk.

Fees

The park charges an entrance fee of $2 per car.

Points of Interest

Big Oak Trail lies between the western shore of the Suwannee and the eastern shore of the Withlacoochee, but several shorter trails start near the park office east of the Suwannee. Suwannee River and Balanced Rock Trails parallel the eastern shore of the river, while Lime Sink Run and Sandhills Trails take the hiker into the interior of the park. Another trail begins at the park office and winds through the remains of Confederate earthworks to an old ferry landing where the town of Columbus once stood.

Columbus was the end of the line for steamboats bringing in

supplies from Cedar Key. The town died when railroads replaced steamboats in northern Florida. Across the river from Columbus was the logging town of Ellaville, which vanished when the trees on which it depended were logged out.

Additional Reading

The De Soto Chronicles, volume 1, edited by Lawrence A. Clayton, Vernon James Knight, Jr., and Edward C. Moore, University of Alabama Press, Tuscaloosa, 1993.

A Naturalist in Florida: A Celebration of Eden by Archie Carr, edited by Marjorie Harris Carr, Yale University Press, New Haven, Connecticut, 1994.

Palmetto Journal: Walks in the Natural Areas of South Carolina by Phillip Manning, John F. Blair, Publisher, Winston-Salem, North Carolina, 1995. The chapter "Along the Fall Line" includes a treatment of cut-and-run logging in the South after the Civil War.

Speaking for Nature by Paul Brooks, Sierra Club Books, San Francisco, 1983. This book was originally published by Houghton Mifflin in 1980.

"Spring" by Henry David Thoreau, in *Walden and the Essay on Civil Disobedience*, Lancer Books, New York, 1968. The essays in *Walden*, including "Spring," were originally published in 1854.

Whose Woods These Are: The Story of the National Forests by Michael Frome, Doubleday and Company, Garden City, New York, 1962.

PANHANDLE

This plain is mostly a forest of the great long-leaved pine
(Pinus palustris Linn.) [T]he earth [is] covered with grass . . .
sparkling with ponds of water.

WILLIAM BARTRAM, 1791

A Forest Redux

Bear Lake Loop Trail
Blackwater River State Forest

Blackwater River State Forest's 183,650 acres sprawl across the northwestern tip of the Panhandle. They adjoin Alabama's Conecuh National Forest to the north. Together, the two make up the largest tract of longleaf-pine forest in the South and probably the world. S.R. 191 traverses the state forest from north to south, S.R. 4 from east to west. The forest's headquarters are located in the village of Munson at the intersection of the two roads.

This walk starts at Bear Lake Recreation Area, which is just off S.R. 4 about 2 miles east of Munson. To walk the trail clockwise (as we did), go left from the parking lot. The path crosses a dam and proceeds northeast along the shore of the lake. After 3 miles, Bear Lake Loop Trail intersects Sweetwater Trail. Proceed 0.1 mile on Sweetwater Trail to a fine longleaf-pine savanna. At the first dirt road, turn around and retrace your footsteps to Bear Lake Loop Trail. It is 1 mile back to the recreation area from there.

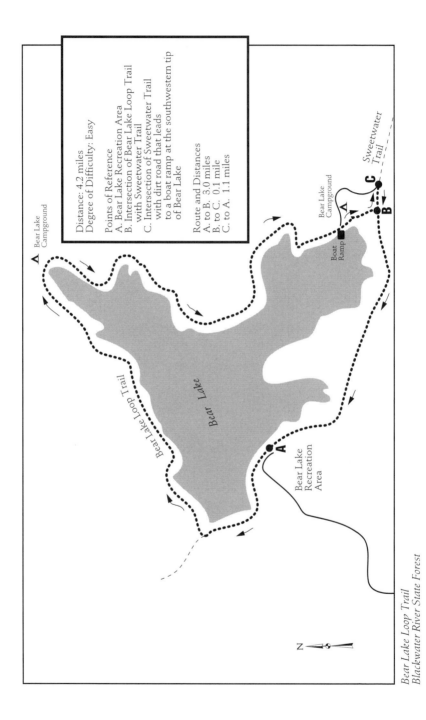

Distance: 4.2 miles
Degree of Difficulty: Easy

Points of Reference
A. Bear Lake Recreation Area
B. Intersection of Bear Lake Loop Trail
   with Sweetwater Trail
C. Intersection of Sweetwater Trail
   with dirt road that leads
   to a boat ramp at the southwestern tip
   of Bear Lake

Route and Distances
A. to B.   3.0 miles
B. to C.   0.1 mile
C. to A.   1.1 miles

Bear Lake Campground

Sweetwater
Trail

Bear Lake
Campground

Boat
Ramp

C

B

A

Bear Lake Loop Trail

Bear   Lake

Bear Lake
Recreation
Area

N

Bear Lake Loop Trail
Blackwater River State Forest

Vernon Compton is a tall man wearing jeans and a faded flannel shirt. He is the forestry resource administrator for Blackwater River State Forest. We are in his office in Munson, a speck of a town in northwestern Florida surrounded by a vast forest of longleaf pines. I have spent an afternoon among those pines, scouting trails for tomorrow's walk, and we are talking about—what else?—longleaf pines.

"Compared to some I've seen, the trees here seem a tad spindly," I say.

"They're young," says Compton. "Longleaf pines can live for five hundred years. Most of these are sixty years old."

"There are no old-growth stands anywhere in Blackwater River?"

Compton looks like a man who's heard all this before. "Let me show you something," he says, digging into the gray file cabinet behind him.

He plops an aerial survey photograph on the desk and shoves it toward me. He points to a half-dozen buildings in the center of the photograph. "That was Munson in the 1930s. Look at the land around it."

I study the photograph. It shows a wasteland of scrub and bare soil. Not a tree is standing except for a fringe of hardwoods along a creek.

"Damn," I whisper.

Compton leans back in his chair. "That's what we had when we started here," he says. "We're proud of what we've accomplished. It wasn't simple, you know; this ecosystem is more complicated than you might think."

The next morning is cool and cloudless. Tree swallows sweep back and forth across Bear Lake. A breeze brings a whiff of sweet-smelling wood smoke and ripples the dark waters of the lake, making them sparkle in the midwinter sun. Dark green pines rim the lake, and a blue jay scolds us from its perch on the railing of a short fishing pier. We follow the blue-blazed Bear Lake Loop Trail out of the recreation area, across a dam, and into the pines.

Most of the trees are about the same size, and they are bunched together more thickly than one would expect in an ideal pine savanna. They are mainly longleaf pines (*Pinus palustris*), but a few show patches of orange bark that identify them as slash pines, which were introduced here about thirty-five years ago. The bark of every tree is charred. Though a few larger pines grow among them, these aren't the towering pines of an old-growth forest. Still, they are sizable enough to make a person who fancies such forests feel at home.

Beneath the pines grow leafless turkey oaks and scattered bunches of yellow-green wire grass. Raccoon and deer tracks dimple the thin layer of sand that covers the clay soil, and purple wildflowers, which Diane identifies as Florida violets, grow beside the path. We pass a group of larger pines marked with white blazes. I study each tree and finally spot a hole fifty or sixty feet above the ground with white sap drippings around it. It is the nesting cavity of a red-cockaded woodpecker, the most famous inhabitant of this forest.

The red-cockaded woodpecker (*Picoides borealis*) is a zebra-backed woodpecker slightly smaller than a robin with a black cap and white cheeks. On each side of its head, the male sports a "cockade," which is actually a tiny, nearly invisible patch of red. Surprisingly, this little bird is driving the renaissance of a great Southern ecosystem.

Congress passed the first law protecting endangered species in 1966, and the red-cockaded woodpecker was put on the list in 1968. The 1966 law was toothless, but it evolved into the much stronger Endangered Species Act of 1973. Suddenly, the red-cockaded woodpecker had powerful friends.

The United States Fish and Wildlife Service appointed a team to draft a recovery plan. Everyone knew *why* the red-cockaded woodpecker was endangered. The bird was a specialist that lived only in old-growth Southern pine forests, and those forests were vanishing. Almost all of the sixty or so million acres of longleaf-pine savannas that covered much of the South's pre-European coastal plain had been destroyed, first by "tar heels" who bled the pines for their resin, then by loggers. In the late 1800s, Florida had 6.5 billion board feet of virgin longleaf pine; forty years later, it had almost none. To save the red-cockaded woodpecker from extinction, some of the South's once-extensive old-growth pine forests would have to be restored.

In this part of the Panhandle, the government was ahead of the curve. The area that is now Blackwater River State Forest was acquired by the United States Department of Agriculture in the 1930s. The idea was to resettle folks who were trying to eke out a living in that destroyed landscape. The government leased the property to the state in 1938. State foresters cleared the land of hardwoods but spared the few remaining longleaf pines to reseed the barren acres naturally. By the time the federal government transferred title to the state in 1954, pines were reclaiming the land. Some stands have been logged and replanted, but others—such as the even-aged pine forest along Bear Lake Loop Trail, with its sprinkling of older, larger seed pines—have not been cut since the 1930s.

The trail crosses several small streams that feed the lake. Along the banks grow titi and gallberry bushes and fragrant sweet bays that perfume the air. A short side trail leads to a pitcher-plant bog. Hawks and crows cry out from the forest, and three wood ducks flush from the lake. The hammering of woodpeckers accompanies us as we walk, but when I finally get my binoculars on one, it isn't a red-cockaded but a red-bellied. The smell of smoke grows stronger.

At the northeastern end of the lake, a boardwalk leads across a marshy pond enclosed by longleaf pines. Gnawed-off trunks of red maples stand in the shallow water. Although beavers obviously live nearby, I can't spot their lodge. Our footsteps disturb two great blue herons, which flap away, croaking their displeasure. Six egrets appear over the lake, gleaming like diamonds in the morning sun.

The trail turns south. The ground between trail and lake is charred black. Wisps of smoke rise from still-smoldering fires, which Vernon Compton said were set earlier in the week.

It is well known that pine savannas require periodic surface fires, ideally every three to five years. Without them, oaks will grow and shade out the young pines, and a hardwood forest will gradually replace the savanna. What is not so well known is the role wire grass plays in these fires—and vice versa.

Wire grass (*Aristida stricta*) has fine, wirelike leaves. It grows in dense tussocks that are a peculiar mixture of yellows and greens and browns. Unlike the verdant grasses in our front yards, living wire grass is a dull yellow-green. Its nondescript color is due to a high percentage of woody cells in its leaves. Furthermore, dead leaves can remain standing in a tussock for years, further muting the color. The high proportion of woody cells and dead leaves makes a clump of wire grass extremely flammable. And when dead pine needles are added to the mix, you have a fire waiting to happen. Which is precisely what the fire-dependent longleaf-pine community needs.

Wire grass has another peculiarity: although it quickly sprouts back from its roots after a fire and often flowers, it is notoriously reluctant to set seed. Until recently, foresters at Blackwater River and throughout the South usually burned longleaf-pine savannas in the winter or early spring, when the fires were easier to control. Those fires reduced hardwoods as expected, but the wire grass did not thrive after burning. As the wire grass diminished, so did the fuel for the next fire. This made the savannas hard to burn on the three-to-five-year cycle required to suppress hardwoods. The result was a pine forest with a hardwood understory, often turkey oaks, exactly the landscape we saw at the beginning of the trail.

Near the southeastern tip of the lake, Bear Lake Loop Trail intersects Sweetwater Trail. We follow the latter east. Tiny orange wildflowers grow beside the path, and the pines are more scattered. The understory is almost pure wire grass, yellow-green and swaying in the breeze. This is classic longleaf-pine savanna.

I love this landscape—the pines, the grass, the black lake. It reminds me of a longleaf-pine savanna described over two hundred years ago by a man who was as taken with this kind of country as I am. In 1773, William Bartram was passing near Augusta, Georgia, when he encountered a pine savanna: "We find ourselves on the entrance of a vast plain . . . [which] is mostly a forest of the great long-leaved pine (Pinus palustris Linn.) [T]he earth [is] covered with grass, interspersed with an infinite variety of herbaceous plants, and embellished with extensive savannas, always green, sparkling with ponds of water."

The grass Bartram mentioned was wire grass, once the most abundant grass on the Southern coastal plain. I wade into the savanna in front of me, through knee-high bunches of it. Clearly, wire grass is flourishing in parts of Blackwater River State Forest. One reason for its resurgence is that ecologists finally figured out how to make this intractable plant set seed.

The longleaf pine–wire grass community evolved in the South, where lightning strikes are common in late spring and summer, the heart of the growing season. Because wire-grass seeds need bare ground to sprout, the plant produces seeds only after a fire. And since natural fires ordinarily occur in late spring and summer, the plant only sets seed after fires in those seasons. To promote the growth of wire grass, Blackwater River's foresters now conduct about 25 percent of their burns in the summer. The result is picture-perfect longleaf-pine savannas like this one.

We retrace our footsteps on Sweetwater Trail, heading back toward the lake for the last leg of our walk. A deep, staccato rapping comes from the pines near the lake. Although I have been looking for red-cockaded woodpeckers, I know that a noise this loud could come only from its much larger cousin, a pileated woodpecker. The sound grows louder, and we follow it to the shore of the lake. I train my binoculars on the source, expecting to see the great flaming crest and powerful bill of a pileated attacking the bark of a pine. Instead, I see a small black-and-white woodpecker hammering away on a hollow tree trunk that reverberates like a drum, magnifying the sound out of all proportion to the bird's size. I study it as it moves around the snag, but it's easy to identify. There's no mistaking the zebra back and white cheek pouches of a red-cockaded woodpecker.

I shouldn't have been surprised at the booming noise it produced. Red-cockaded woodpeckers are hard-pecking little critters. Unlike other woodpeckers, which carve their nests out of rotten, easily excavated trees, red-cockaded woodpeckers drill their nesting cavities in the hard trunks of live pines. Why? The reason goes back to the essence of this forest: fire. Dead pines are far more likely to burn in a surface fire than living trees. So where do pine-loving woodpeckers nest? In live pines, of course.

They invariably choose older pines seventy or more years of age, such as the seed pines left by the loggers at Blackwater River. Older trees are often afflicted with red heart, a fungal disease that attacks and softens the heartwood, making the red-cockaded woodpecker's job easier. Nonetheless, excavating a nest is a daunting task that takes a year or more.

These birds also find their food on older trees. The bugs on which they feed hide in the cracks and crevices of pine bark. In young pines, the bark clings tightly to the trunk, providing few places for insects to live. But in older trees, the bark forms large, loose plates beneath which lurk swarms of the ants and beetles and spiders favored by red-cockaded woodpeckers. Without old-growth pine forests in which to nest and forage, these birds cannot survive—which is the problem of being a specialist during a period of rapid habitat change.

Toward the end of the walk, Bear Lake Loop Trail veers away from the lake. Birds call from the trees, and a great black butterfly wobbles down the trail toward us. The path then turns north and ends in the picnic area. A boy is fishing on the pier. While Diane takes pictures, I stroll over to watch him.

To my astonishment, and his, he pulls in a tiny sunfish, which flops vigorously on the pier. Since he doesn't seem to know what to do with the fish, I unhook it and, without thinking, drop it back into the lake.

The boy, a towhead of about twelve, looks angry. "Hey, that was my fish."

"Sorry," I say, "but he was too small to eat. Let him grow up."

"I'm fishing for bass anyway," says the boy.

"Maybe a bass will eat him."

"Then I catch the bass and eat *him*," he says, with a boy's intuitive knowledge of the food chain.

"Interdependency," I say. "You depend on the bass, the bass on the sunfish, the sunfish on insects. But without the bass, there would be too many sunfish and too few insects. So the insects depend on the bass, too. That's the way ecosystems work."

The boy looks at me as if I'm some kind of a nut, then turns away and threads another worm on his hook.

Ecosystems are called "communities" for good reason: no species exists in isolation. We are all dependent on one another, sometimes in strange, hard-to-fathom ways. Without regular fires, there are no longleaf pines; without longleaf pines, there are no red-cockaded woodpeckers; and without wire grass to fuel them, there are fewer fires. Therefore, the red-cockaded woodpecker depends on the presence of wire grass. Of course, the wire grass depends on fire to set seed. Etc., etc., etc.

Vernon Compton called this ecosystem complicated, and he was right. To save the red-cockaded woodpecker, as mandated by the Endangered Species Act, we must save an entire ecosystem. Which is why federal and state officials are trying to reestablish old-growth longleaf-pine forests throughout the South. It is also why that much-maligned law makes so much sense. "To keep every cog and wheel is the first precaution of intelligent tinkering," wrote Aldo Leopold. And he was right, too.

BEFORE YOU GO

For More Information
Blackwater River State Forest
11650 Munson Highway
Milton, FL 32570
(904) 957-4201

Accommodations
The closest accommodations are in Crestview and Milton, both
of which are about 20 miles from the trailhead. Contact

Crestview Chamber of Commerce
502 South Main Street
Crestview, FL 32536
(904) 682-3212

Santa Rosa County Chamber of Commerce
5247 Stewart Street
Milton, FL 32570
(904) 623-2339

Campgrounds
Four improved and five primitive campgrounds are scattered
through the forest, including one at Bear Lake Recreation Area,

the starting point for this walk. For more information, contact Blackwater River State Forest.

Maps

A map of Bear Lake Loop Trail is available at no charge from the state forest. A map of the entire forest, a necessity for navigating the back roads, is in the free brochure *Blackwater River State Forest.*

Fees

Entrance to Blackwater River State Forest and most of its recreation areas is free. A fee is charged at Krul Recreation Area.

Points of Interest

In addition to Bear Lake Loop, Blackwater River has other hiking trails. Sweetwater Trail runs for 4.5 miles between Krul Recreation Area and Jackson Red Ground Trail, a 21-mile path that crosses the entire forest.

However, the trail I most wanted to walk was Wiregrass Trail. It starts near Hurricane Lake and follows the Blackwater River south for 5.2 miles to Jackson Red Ground Trail. As its name implies, it passes through a longleaf pine–wire grass savanna that is probably not much different from the one we saw on Bear Lake Loop Trail. Because of its proximity to the river, though, this trail is more diverse, offering views of the river and the bottom-land forest along its banks.

Wiregrass Trail and, to a lesser extent, Sweetwater and Jackson Red Ground Trails were damaged by Hurricane Opal, which blew through Blackwater River State Forest in October 1995, a few months before our visit. Downed trees made Wiregrass Trail impassable, but I explored parts of it and concluded that I'd like to walk it when the path is cleared.

During our stay, forest-service crews were removing downed trees throughout Blackwater River, and all trails should be cleared soon.

Additional Reading

"Born of Fire, Under Fire: Understanding the Plight of the Red-cockaded Woodpecker" by Jerome A. Jackson, *Birder's World* 7, December 1993, 12–16.

"The Fiery Story of Wiregrass" by Lawrence S. Earley, *Wildlife in North Carolina* 58, July 1994, 2–3.

"Florida's High-Pine Sandhill Communities" by Henry R. Mushinsky, with an introduction by Hugh Boyter, *Florida Wildlife* 47, May–June 1993, 19–23.

"Florida Uplands: Longleaf Pine Forests" by D. Bruce Means, *Florida Wildlife* 48, September–October 1994, 2–6.

"Longleaf Pine: A Southern Revival" by Tom Horton, *Audubon* 97, March–April 1995, 74–80.

"Restoring a 'Grassroots' Forest" by Carolee Boyles-Sprenkel, *American Forests* 99, May–June 1993, 43–45.

A Stillness in the Pines: The Ecology of the Red-Cockaded Woodpecker by Robert W. McFarlane, W. W. Norton and Company, New York, 1992.

Travels of William Bartram by William Bartram, edited by Mark Van Doren, Dover Publications, New York, 1955. This book was originally published in Philadelphia in 1791 under the title *Travels through North & South Carolina, Georgia, East & West Florida, the Cherokee Country, the Extensive Territories of the Muscogulges, or Creek Confederacy, and the Country of the Chactaws.*

River Bluffs, Ravines, and Disappearing Trees

Torreya Trail
Torreya State Park

The 2,535-acre Torreya State Park is located on the eastern bank of the Apalachicola River about 14 miles northeast of Bristol. C.R. 1641 leads into the park. This walk starts at a parking lot near the entrance gate.

A 25-yard access trail leads south from the parking lot to the white-blazed Torreya Trail. To walk the trail clockwise, as we did, go right at the junction. The trail starts in pine flatwoods, proceeds west to Rock Bluff Primitive Camp, which overlooks the Apalachicola River, then turns north.

At 2.4 miles, a blue-blazed cutoff trail forks east off Torreya Trail. If you continue straight, you will complete the entire 6.3-mile Torreya Trail loop. But when the Apalachicola River is high, the northernmost part of the loop may be underwater, as it was when we were there. Consequently, we took the 1-mile cutoff trail, which passes through a picnic area, then rejoins Torreya Trail. From that junction, it is 2.3 hilly miles back to the trailhead.

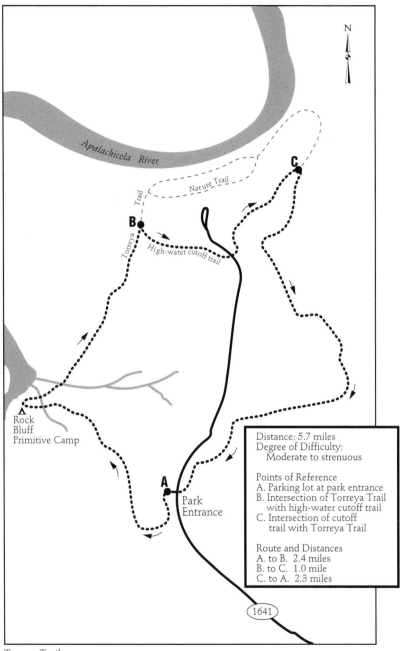

N

Apalachicola River

Nature Trail

C

B

Torreya Trail

High-water cutoff trail

Rock
Bluff
Primitive Camp

A

Park
Entrance

Distance: 5.7 miles
Degree of Difficulty:
  Moderate to strenuous

Points of Reference
A. Parking lot at park entrance
B. Intersection of Torreya Trail
  with high-water cutoff trail
C. Intersection of cutoff
  trail with Torreya Trail

Route and Distances
A. to B. 2.4 miles
B. to C. 1.0 mile
C. to A. 2.3 miles

1641

Torreya Trail
Torreya State Park

Anne Harvey is a compact woman dressed in a damp green uniform. She is manager of Torreya State Park. Her years at the park have apparently accustomed her to its nuisances, because she ignores the late-winter drizzle we are standing in and seems immune to the mosquitoes swarming about her. "So you want to see a Florida torreya? Follow me."

I scratch and slap my way to her pickup. We get out near the entrance to the park's campground. "There it is," she says. I peer through misty rain at a scrawny, dark green tree. It is about twenty feet tall, with a trunk that is less than twelve inches around. It is one of the world's rarest trees; only fifteen hundred or so still survive in the wild, all of them along a thirty-five-mile stretch of the Apalachicola River and most of them on its eastern bank. Of those, about one-third are in Torreya State Park.

The needles are sharp to the touch. I am tempted to break off a few and smell them. When crushed, they are supposed to give off an unpleasant odor, from which the tree gets its other common name, "stinking cedar."

"Every needle is precious," Harvey says, perhaps reading my mind. "*Torreya taxifolia* keeps its needles for up to seven years, unlike a pine, which drops them every year or two."

I yank my hand away and slap another mosquito. "I've read that torreyas will soon be extinct in the wild."

"Yes. They are being attacked by pathogens that are slowly killing them off. So far, no one has come up with a way to stop it."

As we start back to the pickup, I ask the question I most want answered: "Why is this species found only here, along the Apalachicola?"

"That," she says with a smile, "is a long story."

It's eight o'clock in the morning, cloudy, temperature forty-eight degrees. Diane and I are heading for the park, passing seemingly endless pine plantations. The rain has stopped, but it has already messed up the walk I had in mind: the entire Torreya Trail. Anne Harvey told me yesterday that the river was seven feet above flood stage and that the northern part of the trail was underwater. She suggested we use a cutoff trail to avoid that section, and we plan to take her advice.

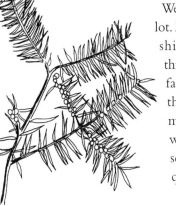

We pull into the trailhead parking lot. Mosquitoes dive-bomb the windshield, trying to eat their way through it. Diane daintily dabs her face with repellent; remembering the hordes of yesterday, I *slather* myself with the stuff. We follow the white-blazed Torreya Trail into a scrubby upland-pine forest. Mosquitoes follow Diane and chew on everything but her face. She stops and bathes in repellent. The mosquitoes vanish, and a mockingbird begins to sing in a nearby pine.

Clumps of wire grass grow beneath fire-charred longleaf pines and leafless turkey oaks. Deer tracks describe intricate patterns in the sandy soil, winding among young pines still in the candle stage. So far, Torreya State Park, often called "Florida's most unusual park," seems quite ordinary.

A moment later, that impression vanishes. The sandy path turns into a hard limestone track, which dips into a ravine maybe forty feet deep, with steep red walls. The terrain looks more like Utah's red-rock country than a Florida upland-pine community.

The trail bends around the head of another ravine. This one is even deeper. Its walls resemble those of a canyon, but it isn't shaped like a canyon. It's shaped like a huge amphitheater dug out of sandstone and red clay. We walk down into it on what is probably the steepest path in Florida.

How these ravines formed is one chapter in Anne Harvey's long story. Surface erosion creates most ravines. A stream washes debris downhill and cuts into the rock or soil over which it flows. If the erosion goes on long enough, the result is a deep gorge such as the Grand Canyon.

Torreya's ravines are not shaped like canyons because they were formed by below-ground erosion. When water flows along an underground slope, it undercuts the ground above it, which then collapses and creates oval-shaped ravines like the ones found along this part of the Apalachicola River. At the bottom of the ravines, one can usually find the streams that created them. (For a more detailed treatment of this topic, see "More about Ravines" at the end of this chapter.)

As we descend into the ravine, the vegetation changes dramatically. Pines and oaks thrive in the dry, sandy soil on the rim and the upper slopes. But oaks, magnolias, and beeches grow on the moist, cool lower slopes and at the bottom of the ravine. Some of these are sizable trees, their crowns at eye level and their bases fifty or more feet below. Beneath the canopy, in the shade and along a cooling stream, are smaller trees usually associated with the southern Appalachian mountains: rhododendron, American holly, and mountain laurel. The torreya tree and the Florida yew (*Taxus floridana*) also grow here, but we fail to spot them.

The trail climbs out of the ravine and continues west. The hardwood forests of the ravines—called "slope forests" by ecologists—alternate with flat, sandy stretches of land thick with pines and scrub oaks. Purple wildflowers brighten the ground beneath the pines, and two crows call raucously overhead. We wade through a patch of red buckeye, then the ground falls away. Over fifty feet below us is the river—sinuous, brown-green, and well above its banks.

The Apalachicola is Florida's most unusual river. It is the only one that originates outside the coastal plain. It starts as the Chattahoochee River, which tumbles out of the Appalachian Mountains in northern Georgia. The Chattahoochee joins the Flint River, which rises in the Piedmont, at Lake Seminole, just north of the Georgia-Florida border. South of the lake, the river is known as the Apalachicola.

One of the Apalachicola's peculiarities is its bluffs, and their origin is another chapter in the region's long story. The Apalachicola River Valley began to form eighteen million years ago, only a few million years after Florida first emerged from the sea. Though much of the Panhandle south of Torreya State Park (and virtually all of peninsular Florida) would be inundated by rising seas many times, the land to the north would never again be underwater. During those eighteen million years, the Apalachicola cut bluffs into its limestone riverbed, some of which now rise as much as 150 feet above the river.

From the top of Rock Bluff, where we are standing, another peculiarity of the Apalachicola is obvious. Though there are sheer bluffs below and on either side of us, the land on the far side of the river slopes gently to the water's edge. It turns out that the Apalachicola's bluffs are found only on the eastern bank of the river.

The reason for this is a tilt in the limestone riverbed. The formation slants downward from west to east. Thus, the river tends to migrate eastward. The migration undercuts the older bluffs on the eastern bank, which eventually collapse, creating new bluffs. The western bank suffers more gradual erosion as the river migrates away from it, forming terraces, which in time erode into gently sloping bottom lands.

Most of the ravines along the river are also on the eastern bank. The seepage streams that create ravines are formed when the river cuts beneath the water table of the surrounding land. Water then seeps out of the valley walls into the river, and an underground stream begins to flow. A seepage-stream ravine will form only when the stream is below the surface of the ground. Since the eastern bank is elevated above the river (and the seepage streams) and the western bank is not, the eastern bank is where ravines form.

From Rock Bluff, Torreya Trail goes downhill. At the bottom of the ravine, it vanishes into an expanse of dark water. "So this is what seven feet above flood stage means," mutters Diane.

"No problem," I say, "we'll just bushwhack upstream to get around it."

We beat our way through a bottom-land forest of cypresses, dwarf palmettos, tall sycamores, and dense canebrakes. Needle palms and ferns grow beneath small ironwood trees. After scrambling upstream for ten minutes, we find a ford narrow enough to cross by stepping on cypress knees.

On the other side, a steep trail climbs out of the ravine, passing leafless beeches, evergreen hollies and magnolias, and a fine oak-leaf hydrangea. Trilliums grow beside the path, and a Carolina wren calls from the woods. Like the vegetation, the ups and downs of the trail make this country seem more like the southern Appalachian foothills than Florida. By the time we reach the top of the bluff, we are hot and sweaty. Below us is another flooded ravine.

"No wonder they call this 'Florida's most unusual park,'" says Diane.

"No problem," I say, "we'll just—"

"I know. Bushwhack upstream."

It turns out to be a longer bushwhack. Finally, we give up and take off our boots and wade across the flooded stream. The water feels cool on my feet, and mud squishes pleasantly through my toes. The climb out, though, is just as steep as the previous one.

At the top of the bluff, we find the blue-blazed cutoff trail and follow it east, climbing away from the river. As we walk, spring advances with us. Away from the river, the air is warmer and the hardwoods have begun to leaf out. A robin hops across the path.

The cutoff trail leads across the park road through a picnic area and a youth camp. It then turns north and heads back toward the river. At the river, it rejoins Torreya Trail, which we follow south, walking beside Rock Creek, a crystalline stream flowing over a white-sand bottom.

The trail continues up and down, passing into and out of shallow ravines. Mixed in with the usual beeches and magnolias is a stand of towering sweet gums, their trunks as straight as plumb lines. Mountain laurel flourishes on the slopes of some ravines, and white oaks, uncommon trees in most of Florida, are abundant. Anne Harvey believes this land was last logged over a hundred years ago, and the size of the trees bears her out. The reason it was spared was probably the terrain, which is rugged enough to dampen the ardor of the most enthusiastic logger.

The path plunges into a deeper ravine. A wooden bridge leads across a stream. Down here, near the creek, the air is noticeably cooler. As we start out of the ravine, Diane points out a waist-high dark green shrub. I touch a branch and feel a familiar prickle. It is a Florida torreya.

Because *T. taxifolia* is so rare and its range so limited, botanists have long tried to explain its presence here. The prevailing theory is based on the region's unique bluffs and ravines and on long-term climate changes—which is why Anne Harvey said it was a long story.

Twenty or so million years ago, a more or less continuous cool-weather flora existed across much of North America and East Asia. One member of that flora was the torreya tree (or one of its ancestors), which was widespread at the time. During the Pleistocene, the world heated up between ice ages, and the torreya survived only in cool, moist locations. This explains the disjunct distribution of the world's four *Torreya* species—one in California, one in Japan, another in China, and, of course, one here.

According to the theory, the cold waters pouring out of the Appalachians met the warm Gulf air along this section of the Apalachicola River. A cool fog settled in the river valley and its ravines. This microclimate enabled cool-weather species to hang on here even when the world warmed. Thus, many of the trees and plants commonly found in the southern Appalachians—

beeches, white oaks, buckeyes, trilliums, and mountain laurel—flourish here, as do Florida yews and torreyas.

The theory makes sense. Today, most torreyas are found in deep ravines shaded by dense slope forests and cooled by streams. It also accounts for the trees' scarceness on the western bank of the river, where ravines are rare.

The theory does not explain why the torreya and the yew vanished from the southern Appalachians and other cool locations while beeches, oaks, and mountain laurel survived. Nor does it explain why the tree should be suddenly attacked by pathogens. The first question may never be answered, but spurred by an interest in taxol—an anticancer drug that comes from the bark of the torreya's cousin, the Pacific yew—two scientists recently identified the pathogen that is killing the Florida torreya.

According to Gary Strobel and Jon Clardy, the culprit is a fungus, *Pestalotiopsis microspora*. They believe that the fungus has always been present in torreyas and that the trees' die-off—which started in the 1950s—was caused by changes in the environment. The fungus appears to kill torreyas where moisture levels are low. In humid climates, it doesn't harm them. They speculate that extensive logging in northern Florida's pine forests created a drier climate that doomed the torreyas. Since there's not much chance of putting the pine forests back together again, scientists are studying fungicides to protect the remaining torreya trees.

The trail continues across rolling terrain, dipping into ravines and passing gurgling streams. Mourning doves perch in red maples, and trilliums grow beneath leafless hardwoods. At Stone Bridge, two branches of Rock Creek merge and form a small cascade.

The streams are perfectly clear and cold to the touch. It's a scene that would make a native of the Smoky Mountains feel at home, and it is hard to remember that we are still in Florida.

Toward the end of the walk, the trail climbs away from the ravines and reenters the high-pine ecosystem. The ground is sandy and dry, and just before we reach the car, I spy a prickly pear growing beside the trail. Could Strobel and Clardy be right? Could logging the pine forests have lowered the humidity of this river valley, creating the conditions that are killing the torreyas? On our walk, we noticed that the ravines we entered *were* cool and moist. But that is anecdotal evidence; perhaps they are not as cool and moist as they once were.

Although the park hasn't been logged for years, the pine plantations that surround it are regularly clear-cut. Could this logging have affected the climate in the ravines and along the river? As usual, assigning causal relationships in natural areas is a dicey business. Maybe *P. microspora* is just another sentence in the stinking cedar's long story. Hopefully, it will not be the last.

BEFORE YOU GO

For More Information
Torreya State Park
Route 2, Box 70
Bristol, FL 32321
(904) 643-2674

Accommodations
Motels are as scarce as torreya trees in this part of Florida. The

best bets are the Cherokee Motel in Blountstown and the Snow-bird in Bristol. Both are about 20 miles from the park. Contact

Cherokee Motel
628 West Central Avenue
Blountstown, FL 32424
(904) 674-9973

Snowbird Motel
P.O. Box 1000
Bristol, FL 32321
(904) 643-2330

Campgrounds

Thirty-five campsites are located in a family campground just off the park's main road. Backpackers can use two primitive camp-sites near Torreya Trail; one is at Rock Bluff high above the Apalachicola River, the other at Rock Creek. For more informa-tion, contact the park.

Maps

A free trail map is available from the park.

Fees

The park charges a $2 entrance fee per car.

More about Ravines

Ravines like the ones in Torreya State Park are found in much of the western Panhandle. They are so common, in fact, that ge-ologists have given them names: seepage-stream ravines and steephead ravines. Technically, the two are different.

True steepheads occur south of the Cody Scarp, a fuzzy line

that divides the sand of ancient Gulf beaches from the clay soil to the north. About 5 million years ago, the Gulf of Mexico reached almost to the borders of the park, and its waves deposited huge quantities of sand on that ancient shore. The 50 or so inches of rain that fall on this part of Florida each year percolate quickly through the sand, then collect on a more impermeable layer of clay deep in the ground. When the water begins to flow, the ground above the underground stream collapses and a steephead forms.

Torreya State Park lies just north of the Cody Scarp. Here, the water comes not from collected rainfall but from underground seepage streams. These streams undercut the ground above them, creating the seepage-stream ravines found along Torreya Trail. To the untrained eye, these ravines are identical to the steepheads to the south.

Points of Interest

Few parks have headquarters worth visiting just for their architecture, but Torreya is an exception. Its offices are in the old kitchen of Gregory House, a two-story plantation home built by Jason Gregory in 1849. The house sits atop a bluff overlooking the Apalachicola River. The rooms not used by the park are furnished in the style of the 1850s.

Though the house itself has an interesting history, the best part of the story is how it got to this bluff. Gregory House was originally situated on the western bank of the Apalachicola at Ocheesee Landing, a little downstream of its present location. The family vacated the house in 1916. It housed caretakers for a few years, then stood empty until 1935, when it was disassembled by members of the Civilian Conservation Corps, who marked each piece as they took the structure apart.

The parts were floated across the river, and the house was reassembled on its present site. The job took three years. Over 60 years later, the park rates the structural integrity of the building as "very high."

The good condition of Gregory House—after it was torn apart and put back together—is just one example of the CCC's craftsmanship. Many parks in Florida and the rest of the United States are similarly indebted to that extraordinary organization.

Additional Reading

"The Apalachicola River Bluffs and Ravines." This handout, available at the park office, was prepared by the park for Earth Day 1990. It was excerpted from "Geobotany of the Apalachicola River Region" by Andre F. Clewell, an unpublished paper.

"Florida's Ancient Shores" by Don Stap, *Audubon* 97, May–June 1995, 36–37.

"Geology of the Apalachicola River Area, Northwest Florida" by Walt Schmidt, *Southeastern Geological Society Guidebook No. 25*, October 8, 1983, 1–9.

"Geomorphology of the Apalachicola River Valley" by E. W. Bishop, *Southeastern Geological Society Guidebook No. 25*, October 8, 1983, 56–60.

"Rescuing an Endangered Tree" by Sasha Nemecek, *Scientific American* 274, March 1996, 22. This article is an account of the work by Gary Strobel and Jon Clardy to identify the fungus that is killing the Florida torreya.

"Vascular Plants of Torreya State Park" by Patricia Elliott, 1971. This unpublished manuscript is available at the park office.

Birds, Beasts, and Other Generalists

Peninsula Trail and Gulf Beach
St. Joseph Peninsula State Park

St. Joseph Peninsula State Park occupies 2,516 acres on the northern half of St. Joseph Peninsula, a sliver of sand in the Gulf of Mexico tenuously attached to the mainland at Cape San Blas. To reach the park from U.S. 98, take S.R. 30 west from Apalachicola or south from Port St. Joe. Cape San Blas Road (S.R. 30E), which leads to the park, branches off S.R. 30 about 16 miles west of Apalachicola and 10 miles south of Port St. Joe.

The walk starts in the northern picnic area, which has the closest parking to the trail. Walk north on the main park road past the rental cabins to a gate where Peninsula Trail begins. A sandy road leads up the center of the peninsula through a fine example of coastal scrub. About a mile beyond the gate, the road enters a wilderness preserve. Continue north for 1.5 miles beyond the wilderness-preserve boundary. A distinct but unmarked trail branches off the road and heads west. When it peters out, pick your way through the scrub to an area of breached foredunes. A sandy path leads through the dunes to the beach. Follow the beach south to a boardwalk that will take you into Campground #2. The campground road leads back to the main road and the picnic area.

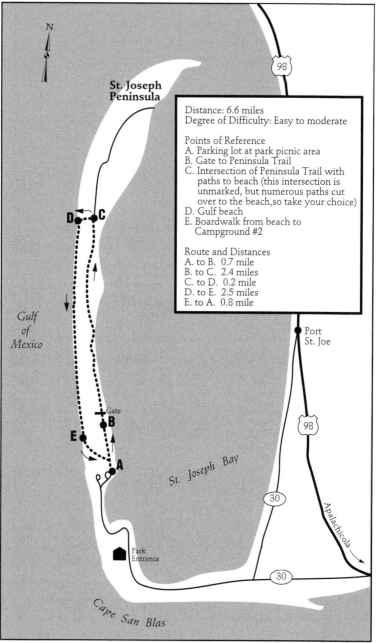

N

St. Joseph Peninsula

Distance: 6.6 miles
Degree of Difficulty: Easy to moderate

Points of Reference
A. Parking lot at park picnic area
B. Gate to Peninsula Trail
C. Intersection of Peninsula Trail with
   paths to beach (this intersection is
   unmarked, but numerous paths cut
   over to the beach, so take your choice)
D. Gulf beach
E. Boardwalk from beach to
   Campground #2

Route and Distances
A. to B. 0.7 mile
B. to C. 2.4 miles
C. to D. 0.2 mile
D. to E. 2.5 miles
E. to A. 0.8 mile

Gulf
of
Mexico

D   C

Port
St. Joe

98

Gate
B

E

A

St. Joseph Bay

30

Apalachicola

Park
Entrance

30

Cape San Blas

Peninsula Trail and Gulf Beach
St. Joseph Peninsula State Park

St. Joseph Peninsula is a fifteen-mile-long forearm of sand running north from its elbow at Cape San Blas to its fingertip at St. Joseph Point. A short biceps of skimpy sand dunes extends east from the elbow, precariously attaching the forearm to the mainland. West of the peninsula is the Gulf of Mexico; to the east is St. Joseph Bay.

The forearm was once an island that emerged from the sea during the last ice age. The biceps that connects it to the mainland formed later. That connection did not survive Hurricane Opal in 1995. The sea washed over Cape San Blas Road and damaged several beach houses. For ten days, until county workers closed the breach, St. Joseph Peninsula was an island again.

From a distance, all of St. Joseph Peninsula appears as pregnable as its biceps, a low ribbon of sand rising out of the Gulf of Mexico. But closer scrutiny dispels that impression. St. Joseph Peninsula State Park, at the northern end of the peninsula, is substantial and stable. Huge dunes protect a thriving scrub forest of sand pines and oaks. Deer and coyotes roam the land, birds flit through the trees, and sea dwellers fill the shallow waters of bay and Gulf. In contrast to the beat-up houses and washed-out road to the south, the park and its inhabitants are doing just fine.

It is a perfect March morning: cool but not cold, bright sun, cloudless sky. I leave the picnic area and walk north on the main park road. Cars cruise by, and wood smoke rises from a campground. Beside the road, two birders alternately peer through a spotting scope.

When I reach the gate where the road ends and Peninsula Trail begins, I duck under it and enter a deserted world. The trail, a sandy fire road, gleams white in the slanting sunlight. Sand pines and wax myrtles and Florida rosemaries line the old road. Beneath them grow saw palmettos and a gray mattress of reindeer moss. Neither Gulf nor bay is visible from the road, but deer tracks are everywhere.

A mockingbird perched in the top of a scrub oak sings ever-changing songs. Two bright red cardinals stand out among the dull needles of a sand pine, and towhees scrabble in the dry leaves that cover the ground between patches of white sand. Dozens of sparrow-sized warblers zip through the pines, drab blurs that flash occasional patches of yellow. When one stops long enough for me to get my binoculars on it, I see a brown body and light breast with a tiny patch of yellow over the wings. When it flies, another yellow patch shows just above the tail. No doubt about it, these are yellow-rumped warblers, and the trees are alive with them.

Yellow-rumped warblers used to be divided into two species: the myrtle warbler, which was primarily an Eastern bird, and Audubon's warbler in the West. In 1973, the two were combined into a single widespread species, *Dendroica coronata*, the yellow-rumped warbler. Because it is so numerous and so easy to identify, the yellow-rump is one of my favorite warblers.

The populations of many songbirds, including warblers, are declining throughout the United States. The fragmentation of breeding habitat and the destruction of the Southern forests where they winter are most often blamed for the decline. The yellow-rumped warbler, however, is holding its own. In bird counts, yellow-rumps often outnumber all other warblers combined. Nonetheless, we will probably never again see a flight like the one recorded by a correspondent of ornithologist Arthur Cleveland Bent. On March 4, 1920, Charles L. Whittle estimated he saw twenty-four thousand yellow-rumped warblers in one day at Sullivan's Island, South Carolina.

The yellow-rump's secret of success lies in its flexibility. It will live almost anywhere as long as a few conifers are present. Even scraggly sand pines such as those along Peninsula Trail will do. Contrast this relaxed habitat requirement to that of the highly specialized red-cockaded woodpecker, which will nest *only* in large, nearly pure stands of old-growth pines. The demise of those forests landed the red-cockaded woodpecker on the endangered-species list but affected the yellow-rumped warbler not at all. In fact, yellow-rumps have been spotted nesting in the least-hospitable forests in North America, Christmas tree farms.

D. *coronata* consumes an amazingly wide range of foods, from the berries of red cedars, dogwoods, and poison ivy to the seeds of sunflowers and goldenrods; from caterpillars, beetles, and weevils to plant-lice eggs and larvae. It also sips sap from sapsucker holes and drinks the juice of fallen oranges. Because of its catholic diet and willingness to live almost anywhere, the yellow-rumped warbler is prospering.

I continue north on the old road and enter the wilderness preserve. In places, the sand is deep enough to make for hard slogging. It's also deep enough to record the comings and goings of animals. In addition to the ubiquitous deer tracks, shallow sine waves mark the passage of snakes, and the imprints of long-fingered paws show that raccoons have passed this way. So far, I've seen no other people, but the wilderness is not deserted; fresh waffle-patterned boot tracks deep enough to belong to a backpacker go north up the center of the road.

A broad path leads west into the scrub. It looks easy enough to follow, so I leave the road and head across the peninsula toward the Gulf. Deep in the scrub, a new set of tracks appears in the sand. The tracks look like the footprints of large dogs. More likely, they were left by the coyotes that now range this peninsula.

Joe Mitchell, a ranger at the park, believes that coyotes were imported into southern Alabama a few years ago to train dogs for fox hunting. Being crafty beasts, some of them escaped and spread to surrounding regions, including the park. But their inadvertent introduction only hastened a result that was inevitable. Coyotes

have been moving east for years. Today, their nocturnal howls can be heard in every Southern state.

Despite countless campaigns to exterminate them in the West, coyotes have thrived. They succeed for the same reason yellow-rumped warblers do: they are generalists.

Like the yellow-rump, the coyote (*Canis latrans*) will eat almost anything, alive or dead, and it can survive in most North American habitats from Florida scrub to Alaskan taiga. It does well in populated areas, too; I once saw a pair of coyotes cruising down a dry wash in the middle of suburban Tucson, where they snap up homeowners' cats with relish.

In the park, coyotes have been similarly opportunistic. Feral cats, once common here, are now rare. And though the deer herd is large and healthy, coyotes will probably slow its growth by attacking fawns. While few daytime visitors to the park encounter coyotes, backpackers camped at St. Joseph Point regularly hear their wild night music.

I follow the sandy path farther into the scrub. The coyote tracks turn north, but I continue west. Finally, the trail peters out, and I trudge across soft sand, picking my way between thick rosemary bushes and low pines. Dunes loom ahead, but a wash leads between them. I follow it through a break in the dunes and emerge on the firm sand of the beach.

It is nearly windless, and the Gulf is calm, a gray-green pond with only a whisper of surf. A few streaky clouds have moved in, but the rest of the sky is luminous blue. A willet probes the white-sand beach, and sanderlings dance at the water's edge. An osprey circles overhead.

I begin walking south. Arks and cockle shells crunch under my feet, and surf clams and fighting conchs lay half-buried in the sand. Lifeless, nearly transparent cabbage-sized blobs litter the beach near the high-tide line. I sit down beside one and poke its tough skin with my finger. A closer inspection is not necessary; these creatures wash up regularly on Southern beaches, and I've examined them many times before. They are cannonball jellyfish (*Stomolophus meleagris*), and their numbers make the yellow-rumped warbler and the coyote seem like endangered species.

The cannonball jellyfish is one of nine thousand species belonging to the phylum Cnidaria. Many people are unfamiliar with this phylum, and those of us who have had experience with its members have regretted it. The names alone are enough to disturb you: Portuguese man-of-war, fire coral, sea whip, sea nettle. But direct contact is more disturbing.

My encounter with a Portuguese man-of-war was so painful that I wondered if my left hand was going to fall off, and an hour or two later, I wished it would. Another time, I waded into a school of sea nettles and received burning red blisters on my legs that lasted for days. Of course, I should count myself lucky. I could have tangled with a box jellyfish. Box jellies, found off the coast of Australia, are probably the most venomous animals on earth. A large one has enough poison to kill sixty people.

Compared to box jellies, cannonballs are downright friendly. They are only mildly toxic, and if you avoid their short tentacles, they are safe to touch.

Sea turtles, especially leatherbacks, appear to be immune to the stings of jellyfish, and they consume enormous numbers of the creatures. Nevertheless, jellyfish (and their look-alike relatives, the siphonophores) are incredibly abundant. They range from the Arctic Ocean to the Antarctic and are found from the surface to depths of over two thousand feet. Cannonball jellies are especially plentiful in the Gulf of Mexico. One swarm was observed drifting through a channel at the rate of two million per hour.

Cannonball jellyfish will eat whatever floats into their tentacles, from copepods to oyster larvae. Like yellow-rumps and coyotes, they are widespread generalists. This—coupled with their low value as food for humans—has served them well in the face of the pressures we are putting on our oceans. As we eat our way through the world's fisheries, the number of finfish has dropped dramatically, but cannonball jellies are flourishing.

I give the jellyfish a final pat and resume walking down the beach. A huge hunk of metal looms ahead. When I reach it, I see that it is a tank about five feet wide and twenty feet long sitting high on the beach. According to Joe Mitchell, it is part of a dredge that was knocked to pieces by Hurricane Opal. It floated down here from St. Andrews, a state recreation area near Panama City. A ring-billed gull stands on top of the tank like a gladiator lording it over a vanquished opponent. I signal thumbs down, but the gull ignores me.

Near the end of the walk, a boardwalk made of new lumber leads through the dunes to a campground. Beside it are the smashed remains of an older boardwalk, another victim of Hurricane Opal.

As usual, when hurricanes smack barrier islands, they inflict the most damage on things man-made: roads, boardwalks, dredges, and houses. Unlike the park and the generalists that inhabit it, which were almost unharmed by Opal, these rigid structures did not evolve with hurricanes. Though *Homo sapiens* is the ultimate generalist, the specialized constructs we build lack flexibility, and if we weren't around to maintain them, our beach houses and beach roads would soon join the red-cockaded woodpecker on the endangered list.

BEFORE YOU GO

For More Information
   St. Joseph Peninsula State Park
   8899 Cape San Blas Road
   Port St. Joe, FL 32456
   (904) 227-1327

Accommodations
   The park rents eight furnished cabins, any of which would be an ideal base for this walk or for just rambling around St. Joseph

Peninsula. For information, contact the park.

Apalachicola, about 35 miles east of the park, has numerous inns, motels, and bed-and-breakfasts. Port St. Joe is closer but offers a more limited selection. Contact

Apalachicola Bay Chamber of Commerce
84 Market Street
Apalachicola, FL 32320
(904) 653-9419

Gulf County Chamber of Commerce
P.O. Box 964
Port St. Joe, FL 32457
(904) 227-1223

Campgrounds

The park has 119 campsites in two campgrounds. Reservations are accepted. For more information, contact the park.

Backpackers with a permit may camp in the wilderness preserve, with some restrictions; they must pack in everything they will need, including water.

Maps

A free trail map is available from the park, but the peninsula is so slender that it is virtually impossible to get lost.

Fees

The park charges a $3.25 entrance fee per vehicle.

Points of Interest

Every spring and fall, thousands of migrating hawks pass over St. Joseph Peninsula. Because hawks prefer not to fly over water, the narrow peninsula acts as a funnel that concentrates the raptors. This creates an opportunity for great birding. The best times to catch the migration are late September and October, especially after a cold front has passed through. The park publishes a two-page guide, *St. Joseph Peninsula Hawk Migration*, which provides detailed information on the best spots and times to observe migrating hawks.

Additional Reading

"Bound for Deep Water" by Scott A. Eckert, *Natural History*, March 1992, 28–35.

"Deadly Jellyfish of Australia" by William M. Hamner, *National Geographic* 186, 116–30.

"Growing Bigger Coyotes" by Mark Derr, *Audubon* 96, November–December 1994, 20–22.

Life Histories of North American Wood Warblers, part 1, by Arthur Cleveland Bent, Dover Publications, New York, 1963. This book was originally published in 1953 as the Smithsonian Institution's *Bulletin 203*.

"Pulsating Parachutes of the Sea" by Jack and Anne Rudloe, *Smithsonian* 21, February 1991, 100–111. This is the best introduction to the natural history of jellyfish that I have run across.

"Space-Age Jewels" by Cheryl Lyn Dybas, *National Wildlife* 30, August–September 1992, 18–24.

"The Yellow-Rumped Clan" by Matthew Pelikan, *Birder's World* 10, June 1996, 30–34.

A Resilient Land

Stoney Bayou and Deep Creek Trails
St. Marks National Wildlife Refuge

St. Marks National Wildlife Refuge lies along the northern and western shores of Apalachee Bay about 20 miles south of Tallahassee. The refuge covers almost 97,000 acres, one-third of them water. It is divided into three units: Panacea, Wakulla, and St. Marks. This walk is in the St. Marks Unit. To reach this unit from Tallahassee, take S.R. 363 south, then go east on U.S. 98 and south on S.R. 59 (Lighthouse Road). The trailhead is on the eastern side of S.R. 59 about a mile south of the visitor center.

Aucilla Tram Road leads east along a dike. At 1.9 miles, take Stoney Bayou Trail south to a large impoundment. Where Stoney Bayou Trail turns east, proceed straight ahead to Deep Creek Trail, which runs along the edge of a salt marsh, then turns north and rejoins Stoney Bayou Trail. Continue north to Aucilla Tram Road and follow it back to the trailhead.

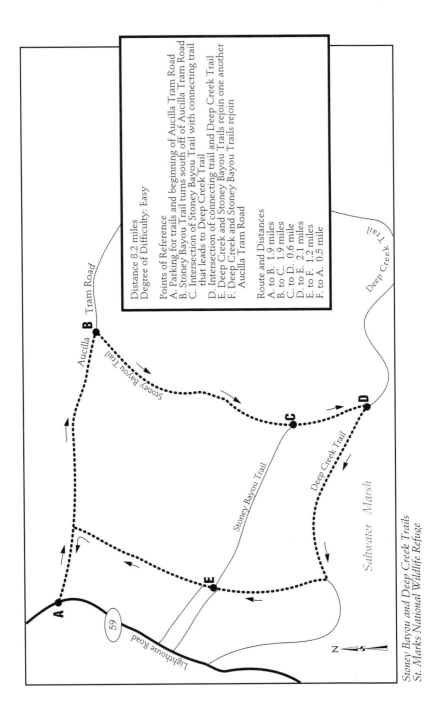

Distance 8.2 miles
Degree of Difficulty: Easy

Points of Reference
A. Parking for trails and beginning of Aucilla Tram Road
B. Stoney Bayou Trail turns south off of Aucilla Tram Road
C. Intersection of Stoney Bayou Trail with connecting trail
   that leads to Deep Creek Trail
D. Intersection of connecting trail and Deep Creek Trail
E. Deep Creek and Stoney Bayou Trails rejoin one another
F. Deep Creek and Stoney Bayou Trails rejoin
   Aucilla Tram Road

Route and Distances
A. to B. 1.9 miles
B. to C. 1.9 miles
C. to D. 0.6 mile
D. to E. 2.1 miles
E. to F. 1.2 miles
F. to A. 0.5 mile

Stoney Bayou and Deep Creek Trails
St. Marks National Wildlife Refuge

If you asked central casting to supply an actor to play the veteran boss of a wildlife refuge, you would probably get a person who looks like Joe White, the manager of St. Marks National Wildlife Refuge. He is of medium height, well built, with gray hair and a craggy, tanned face. After two decades on the job, White is still dazzled by the beauty of the place he manages. Of course, he's been here long enough to be realistic about it, too. He leans back in his chair, props his feet on the desk, looks around his spacious office, and tries to come up with the right word. "*Paradise?*" he says. "Maybe so . . . except, of course, for the fire ants, cattails, and July and August."

"Every natural area is like that," I say. "They aren't perfect places. Yosemite has avalanches; Acadia has black flies; Everglades has mosquitoes."

"Sure," he says. "This place may not be paradise, but it is certainly resilient. And I'll take that any day. This land was logged around the turn of the century and became a cow pasture after that. The refuge wasn't created until 1931, and look at it now. Wild and beautiful. Filled with birds and alligators, bears and bobcats. Of course, it's not completely natural. The Civilian Conservation Corps

built miles of dikes to create freshwater impoundments for migrating waterfowl. But some visitors aren't satisfied with what's
been done. They want more improvements. Maybe get rid of bit-
ing insects, for instance."

"That's where trouble starts," I say. "Exterminating pests in natural
areas often causes more damage than it's worth. And it usually
doesn't work anyway."

"Right," he says. "They're like July and August. You can't get
rid of them, so you might as well learn to live with them."

I start east on Aucilla Tram Road on a warm late-winter day. To
the north are pine flatwoods, dull green beneath a gray sky; to
the south is a marshy field. The road, two tracks separated by a
grassy center strip, stretches out long and straight in front of me.
Canals filled with dark, tannin-stained water line both sides of
the road, and violets, thistles, and blackberries cover the ground
beside them.

Birds are everywhere. The mournful *coo, coo, coo* of doves comes
from the fields, and woodpeckers hammer away in the pines. An
osprey sails overhead, and a prothonotary warbler, a bright yellow
harbinger of spring, flashes through the low brush. Eight great
egrets, ghostly shapes in the overcast sky, appear above the trees
and flap silently toward the marsh.

I leave Aucilla Tram Road and take Stoney Bayou Trail south. A
box turtle plods across the path, and a black swallowtail floats
along the edge of the marsh, stopping to sip nectar from black-
berry blooms. Mounds of gray dirt as big as oversized dinner
plates are spaced forty or so feet apart beside the trail. I avoid

them; I know what lies beneath that crumbly soil. Unfortunately, they are so numerous that I accidentally step on one while trying to watch an osprey. I jerk my foot back and peer down at a seething mass of tiny reddish black ants. They are fire ants, one of the imperfections in Joe White's paradise.

At least one species of fire ant, *Solenopsis geminata*, is native to North America. Its members are found throughout the United States, but they are most numerous in the Southeast and the Southwest. I have been bitten by these native fire ants, and their sharp, stinging bites are indeed fiery. The mounds along Stoney Bayou Trail, however, were made by a different, more fearsome breed. Inside the innocuous gray mounds are thousands of imported fire ants (*S. invicta*), ill-tempered creatures that make our native species seem cuddly.

S. invicta hitchhiked into this country from South America in the 1930s, probably aboard a ship that docked in Mobile, Alabama. The ants spread through the South from Texas to Virginia. Because they are more aggressive than our native ants, they quickly kill them or drive them out. They eat everything from corn to baby birds. And do they ever bite. One biologist said an imported fire-ant bite is like "red hot needles zapping your flesh."

Concern over the spread of South American fire ants in the South escalated to near-hysteria in the 1950s and 1960s. We tackled the problem with our usual hubris. After all, they were mere ants, and we had an arsenal of deadly chemicals at our disposal. First, we tried heptachlor, then mirex. Tons of these pesticides were sprayed on land infested with fire ants. The applications did, in fact, kill the ants, but they also polluted streams and wiped out most native wildlife. Furthermore, fire ants quickly recolonized the treated areas. By the 1970s, both pesticides were banned as a means of fire-ant control. Today, several biologists are forecasting an ecological cataclysm in the South if something isn't done to slow the population growth of imported fire ants.

The ants in the mound I stepped on are settling down. They are not moving as fast as before, and they don't look as belligerent. One by one, they disappear into the nest.

I recall that the introduction of carp into North America elicited a similarly pessimistic response from biologists, many of whom predicted the demise of native freshwater game fisheries. After years of trying to figure out how to get rid of carp, one biologist finally stated the obvious: we can't eliminate these fish, so we might as well learn to live with them. We did, and our game fish survived. And if our ecosystems can adapt to carp, they can probably adapt to fire ants, too.

Stoney Bayou Trail continues south. The overcast has burned off, and the sun warms my shoulders. Jessamine vines have climbed almost every tree and bush along the trail, and their bright yellow flowers are everywhere, perfuming the air. The *keeyer, keeyer, keeyer* of an irritated red-shouldered hawk comes from the pines.

As I walk, puddles of water begin to appear in the marsh. Cypresses replace pines, and the landscape gradually changes from damp ground to a cattail-rimmed open-water impoundment. Herons and egrets stalk the shallows, and blue-winged teals paddle about in the center. Two small gators swim lazily toward us, shadowy shapes with only their eyes above water.

When the CCC built these dikes in the 1930s and 1940s, this part of St. Marks was saltwater marsh. There were no impoundments. The dikes enable the refuge manager to manipulate water levels and salinity to create the open freshwater impoundments favored by wading birds and dabbling ducks.

The impoundments are under constant attack, though. But unlike fire ants, these pests are a native species. Cattails love fresh and mildly brackish water, and if allowed to spread unchecked, they would soon clog the impoundments.

Three species of cattails occur in Florida. The most common is *Typha latifolia*, the broad-leaved cattail. The refuge controls cattails by methods that are simpler and less destructive—and more effective—than those tried on fire ants.

The preferred way is to pump salt water into the impoundments. This shocks the cattails and stops their growth. The other method is to spray cattails with a biodegradable herbicide. This technique is less popular with refuge employees, who must cruise the marshes in a noisy airboat, spraying herbicide under a hot sun. A third method has not, as far as I know, been tried. According to some sources, cattails can be harvested for food and other useful items.

At the height of the back-to-the-land movement of the 1960s and 1970s, the late Euell Gibbons, the enthusiastic eater of almost anything wild, called the cattail the "Supermarket of the Swamps." "For the number of different kinds of food it produces," he said, "there is no plant, wild or domesticated, which tops the common Cattail. . . . In the spring, the young shoots can be yanked from the ground and peeled, leaving a tender white part from six to twelve inches long which may be eaten raw or cooked."

You can shake the pollen from the spikes and eat it, too. You can make flour from the roots of cattails and weave the long, fibrous leaves into all manner of useful things, from baskets to hats. So another method of cattail control might be to invite a bunch of hungry back-to-the-landers to help themselves in a cattail-choked impoundment. It might not be as effective as a dose of salt water or herbicide, but it would probably be more fun for the participants.

Stoney Bayou Trail turns west and parallels the southern edge of the impoundment, but I continue south to Deep Creek Trail, which runs along the outermost dike. Beyond it is salt marsh, a brown and monotonous stand of waist-high needlerush relieved only by an occasional tidal creek and pine island.

The salt marsh is still, but the freshwater impoundment north of the dike teems with life. Ospreys, alligators, warblers, killdeer, and blue-winged teals go about their business in the shallow blue-gray waters. One bird, however, dominates here. Hundreds of red-winged blackbirds, coal black with bright red epaulets, flash back and forth across the water, lighting on cattails, harassing passing hawks, and filling the air with their guttural *checks* and gurgling songs.

Ornithologists have assigned the red-winged blackbird (*Agelaius phoeniceus*) to the family Icteridae, also known as the blackbird family. The nomenclature seems designed to confuse, since all black birds are not blackbirds, and all blackbirds are not black. The all-black American crow, for example, belongs to the family Corvidae, and the European blackbird (of which four and twenty were once served to a king) is a thrush. But the brightly colored Baltimore oriole is a true blackbird.

Blackbirds are a fecund family. Grackles, cowbirds, and orioles are among our most common birds, but the species in this marsh makes them seem rare. Gordon Orians, author of *Blackbirds of the Americas*, said, "The red-winged blackbird may be the most abundant bird in North America."

Blackbirds' abundance has led to conflicts with another abundant species, *Homo sapiens*. In 1667, the Massachusetts Bay Colony passed a law requiring that "every unmarried man . . . shall kill six blackbirds" and "shall not be married until he obeys this order." Another blackbird species, the bobolink, was so destructive to the rice crops of South Carolina that it became known as the "rice bird" and was slaughtered unmercifully to protect that crop. Several states placed bounties on red-wings, mistakenly believing that they "did great damage to grain." So far, no wars have been waged against Florida red-wings, perhaps because they hang around marshes, where they pose no threat to agriculture and are pleasing to watch.

I follow the outer dike west, the seemingly dead salt marsh on one side and the wildlife-packed freshwater marsh on the other. Saltwater marshes are supposed to be among the most productive ecosystems in the world, but they often appear inanimate, as this one does. Occasionally, the quiet is interrupted by the splash of a mullet or the croak of a heron, but what one sees is acre after acre of tall, gray *Juncus roemerianus*, black needlerush.

Both observations are true. Saltwater marsh is a highly productive ecosystem. It can also appear lifeless, especially when compared to a bustling freshwater marsh.

This apparent lifelessness is due to the nature of the food web in saltwater marshes. Periodic flooding by salt water creates a harsh environment in which only a few organisms flourish. Eastern salt marshes are dominated by monotypic stands of *Spartina alterniflora* or *J. roemerianus*. They and the ubiquitous algae are the main food supply for everything that lives in the marsh. The plants are mainly cellulose, however, and few animals can digest cellulose directly. They must wait for plants to die and for bacteria and fungi to break down the cellulose into something tastier. What's left after bacteria attack a blade of dead *J. roemerianus* are tiny particles of food. The creatures that consume these particles are called detritus eaters, and they tend to be small but incredibly numerous.

So despite its appearance, the salt marsh is actually filled with life: grasses and rushes; fungi, algae, and bacteria; grasshoppers, snails, and bugs; crabs, mullet, and oysters. But crabs and snails and such are small, quiet animals, and as you walk beside one of these marshes, it seems silent and still, while the less-specialized freshwater marsh, filled with drinkable water and easily digestible goodies such as cattails, is vibrant with life.

At the end of the impoundment, Deep Creek Trail turns north and heads back toward the trailhead. Sizable gars hang motionless in the canals. A swarm of butterflies—black swallowtails and red-spotted purples—floats up from the side of the path. An osprey stoops and misses a lucky fish in the impoundment.

So much life, seen and unseen, is packed into these marshes and forests that it is hard to remember that much of St. Marks was grassland less than a hundred years ago. Joe White said this is a resilient land, and he was right. Given half a chance, nature will right itself, as it has here at St. Marks—with a little help from the CCC and refuge personnel. And if this land can survive what we humans did to it, it will almost certainly survive fire ants, cattails, and a slew of red-winged blackbirds.

But there's nothing wrong with helping nature when we can. Sometimes, though, we have to accept that we can't solve every problem, and that our solutions may cause more damage than the problem itself. We get into trouble when our hubris won't let us accept our limitations. So there's no need for bounties or pesticides at St. Marks, but an occasional shot of salt water to hold down the cattails is probably a good idea.

BEFORE YOU GO

For More Information
St. Marks National Wildlife Refuge
P.O. Box 68
St. Marks, FL 32355
(904) 925-6121

Accommodations
St. Marks provides a list of hotels, motels, and campgrounds near the refuge. To get a copy, contact the refuge.

Campgrounds
Camping is not permitted in the wildlife refuge except by through-hikers on Florida National Scenic Trail. Contact the ref-

uge for a list of public and private campgrounds in the area.

Maps

St. Marks provides a free map of the refuge. A trail map, "Primitive Walking Trails," shows the details of Stoney Bayou and Deep Creek Trails.

Fees

The refuge charges a $4 entrance fee per vehicle.

Points of Interest

In addition to the trails in the St. Marks Unit, there are good hikes in the refuge's other two units. North Line Road, which runs along the northern border of the Wakulla Unit, passes through a fine hardwood forest. The Panacea Unit's 9-mile Otter Lake Loop takes the hiker through the refuge's pine uplands.

Many miles of dikes and roads crisscross the refuge and are open to hikers. Also, two segments of Florida National Scenic Trail pass through St. Marks; parts of Stoney Bayou and Deep Creek Trails follow the route of this trail.

Additional Reading

"Ants with Attitudes" by Michael J. Killion and S. Bradleigh Vinson, *Wildlife Conservation* 98, January–February 1995, 46–51 and 73.

Blackbirds of the Americas by Gordon H. Orians, University of Washington Press, Seattle, 1985.

"Clash of the Fire Ants" by Janisse Ray, *Florida Wildlife* 49, January–February 1995, 19–21.

Exploring Wild Northwest Florida by Gil Nelson, Pineapple Press, Sarasota, 1995.

Field Guide to Coastal Wetlands Plants of the Southeastern United States by Ralph W. Tiner, University of Massachusetts Press, Amherst, 1993.

"Fire in the Sand" by David S. Lee, *Wildlife in North Carolina* 60, October 1996, 22–25.

Life and Death of the Salt Marsh by John and Mildred Teal, Ballantine Books, New York, 1969.

"Lifestyles of the Rich and Famous" by John Carey, *National Wildlife* 33, December–January 1995, 44–48. This is an article about the blackbird family.

Stalking the Wild Asparagus by Euell Gibbons, David McKay Company, New York, 1962.

Acknowledgments

I am grateful to Diane Manning, who illustrated the book, edited each chapter, and accompanied me on many of the walks. Without her, none of the books in this series would exist.

About twenty-five years ago, two friends and neighbors of ours, Milton and Anne Gillespie, moved from North Carolina to Florida. Because of our inclination to travel south, we've seen more of them since they moved than when they lived a few blocks away.

Year after year, we came to Florida, and year after year, they put us up. They allowed us to use their house as a base to research parts of this book and introduced us to some of the natural areas. They fed us smoked mackerel and deviled eggs and good, cheap rum from Puerto Rico. They took us fishing from Mosquito Lagoon to the Key West flats. Once or twice, we even caught fish. Their hospitality and companionship made our countless trips to Florida more productive and more fun than we had any right to expect.

The Monday Night Writers' Group—Dorrie Casey, Susan Ballenger, Maura Stokes, and Mary Russell Roberson—made their usual constructive suggestions and kept me on the trail when I tried to wander.

If there is a better organization for a writer to work with than John F. Blair, I haven't heard of it. Carolyn Sakowski and her staff know the publishing business, and it is a pleasure to watch them make books out of manuscripts.

Each chapter in the book has its own bibliography, but these bibliographies do not include some of the references that I used almost every day, some in the office and others on the trail.

Audubon Society Field Guides

I own almost every one of these gems. They have proved useful on the trail and off.

The Roger Tory Peterson Field Guide Series

Like most birders in the eastern United States, I rely on *Peterson's Field Guide to the Birds East of the Rockies* when I am afield. Other guides in this series were also useful, especially *Eastern Trees* and *Animal Tracks*.

Ecosystems of Florida, edited by Ronald L. Myers and John J. Ewel, University of Central Florida Press, Orlando, 1990. This book is must reading for anyone interested in Florida's natural communities.

The Trees of Florida by Gil Nelson, Pineapple Press, Sarasota, 1994.

Florida's Birds by Herbert W. Kale, II, and Davis S. Maehr, Pineapple Press, Sarasota, 1990.

Florida Wildlife

I am a subscriber to this magazine, and it is the first place I looked for information on Florida's flora and fauna.

Footprint

This newsletter, published by the Florida Trail Association, contains up-to-date information on the state's trails. The association also helps to maintain many of these trails, including Florida National Scenic Trail. I have been a member of this organization for years, and I encourage anyone interested in exploring the state's natural areas to join. It may be reached at P.O. Box 13708, Gainesville, FL 32604 (800-343-1882).

When I finish a walk, I like to spend time with the people who run our parks and refuges and national forests; the men and women who manage the land and blaze the trails; the folks who band ducks, plant trees, and deal with the public. They are the heroes and heroines of this book, and their work makes it possible for the rest of us to enjoy Florida's natural areas.

Somehow, in addition to their normal duties, these people found time to answer my questions about coontie and reindeer moss, fire ants and roseate spoonbills, otters and coyotes. Many of them vetted chapters, and their comments helped to minimize the inaccuracies that can crop up in a book of nonfiction. The following people helped me with the chapters listed below:

"Victories Big and Small"
Jenny Vasarhelyi, J. N. "Ding" Darling National Wildlife Refuge

"Rock, Water, and Fire"

Roberta D'Amico, Everglades National Park
Rick Cook, Everglades National Park

"Adventures in Engineering"
Tom Hambright, Monroe County's May Hill Russell Library
Ray Thacker, Pigeon Key Foundation
Dan Gallagher, Pigeon Key Foundation
Rick Cook, Everglades National Park

"Birds, Bromeliads, and Field Naturalists"
Andrew J. Mackie, Corkscrew Swamp Sanctuary
Ed Carlson, Corkscrew Swamp Sanctuary

"A Varied but Constant Land"
Paula Benshoff, Myakka River State Park
Jim Igoe

"Climbing Elton's Pyramid"
George Aycrigg, Lake Kissimmee State Park

"Life and Death in the Salt Marsh"
Dorn Whitmore, Merritt Island National Wildlife Refuge

"Big Scrub"
Jim Thorsen, Seminole Ranger District, Ocala National Forest

"A Walk with Billy"
Susan Carl, Paynes Prairie State Preserve

"Old Florida"
Paul Perras, Manatee Springs State Park

"Ecology 101"
Kathleen Hopper, Little Talbot Island State Park

"Songs of the River"
Dave Randall, Suwannee River State Park
Craig Parenteau, Florida Department of Recreation and Parks
Kristy Manning

"A Forest Redux"
Vernon Compton, Blackwater River State Forest

"River Bluffs, Ravines, and Disappearing Trees"
Anne Harvey, Torreya State Park
Mary Russell Roberson

"Birds, Beasts, and Other Generalists"
Anne Harvey, Torreya State Park
Joe Mitchell, St. Joseph Peninsula State Park

"A Resilient Land"
Joe White, St. Marks National Wildlife Refuge
Robin Will, St. Marks National Wildlife Refuge

Finally, though many people helped in the preparation of this book, I alone am responsible for any omissions and errors that remain.

Index